Garden Rooms

THE BEST OF
FINE GARDENING

Garden Rooms

The Taunton Press

Cover photo: David McDonald

Back-cover photos: left, Terrence Moore; top center,
Jesse Cabungcal; bottom center, David McDonald

Back-cover illustration: Rosalind Loeb Wanke

Taunton
BOOKS & VIDEOS
for fellow enthusiasts

First printing: 1996
Printed in the United States of America

A Fine Gardening Book

Fine Gardening® is a trademark of The Taunton Press, Inc.,
registered in the U.S. Patent and Trademark Office.

The Taunton Press
63 South Main Street
Box 5506
Newtown, CT 06470-5506

Library of Congress Cataloging-in-Publication Data

Garden rooms.
        p.   cm. — (The Best of Fine gardening)
    Articles originally published in Fine gardening magazine.
    "A Fine gardening book."
    Includes index.
    ISBN 1-56158-138-0
    1. Landscape gardening. 2. Gardens — Design. 3. Garden
rooms. I. Fine gardening. II. Series.
SB473.G2889   1996   95-45511
712'.6 — dc20   CIP

Contents

Introduction

The idea of applying the concept of "rooms" to outdoor gardens has been around for quite a while. But its popularity has soared lately as the trend toward outdoor living increases, and people search for ways to spend more time actually *in* their yards, not just admiring their gardens from the living-room window. So we thought it was about time to put together this great collection of articles from *Fine Gardening* magazine on designing garden rooms.

In this beautifully photographed volume, expert home gardeners and landscape designers share firsthand accounts of how they created outdoor rooms that are as beautiful as they are functional. Ranging from the tried-and-true to the innovative, many of the approaches recommended by the authors are sure to suit your site.

You'll find the articles in this collection especially helpful and inspiring because they are the work of enthusiasts, gardeners who have given much thought to how they want to integrate their gardens into their daily lives. Sharing their hard-won experience, the authors tell you how to turn your own fantasy retreat into a reality.

The editors of *Fine Gardening* hope you'll experiment with the ideas in this collection of articles. No matter which you choose to try, your efforts will be rewarded.

"The Best of *Fine Gardening*" series collects articles from back issues of *Fine Gardening* magazine. A note on p. 96 gives the date of first publication for each article; product availability, suppliers' addresses and prices may have changed since then. This book is the ninth in the series. The next title is *The Best of* Fine Gardening *on Galleries of Garden Plants.*

Bring privacy and intimacy right to the front door. Walls, a ceiling and a floor make the entry garden an extension of the house's interior.

The Enclosed Entry Garden

Three simple elements turn a public
space into a private haven

by Barbara Ashmun

Remember the old-fashioned parlor, full of fancy furniture, that was reserved for special company, its seats rarely rumpled by people? A lot of entry gardens are like these parlors—public spaces made for show rather than use. As a garden designer, my first job when consulting with homeowners is to help design or redesign the entry garden. My goal is to make it a useful, enjoyable space for the family rather than for the mailman or passersby.

Many front yards are right on the road, exposed to traffic, unsightly views and the curiosity of pedestrians. Almost every gardener I know would prefer a private front yard, yet tradition stops them from having the desired separation from the public. At the same time, living space has become increasingly precious as builders cram more and bigger houses onto smaller lots. As the size of the back yard shrinks, so does the outdoor space homeowners have in which to entertain, dine and garden peacefully.

By enclosing the entry to make it a private garden room, many benefits result. You can extend your home's living space to relax as you please. You can salvage valuable sunny exposure for a private place to grow flowers, vegetables or fruit. You can create views to enjoy from inside your house. The enclosing walls of your garden will not only look beautiful, but they will also screen out unsightly areas and reduce road noise, and they can serve as a backdrop for plants.

An enclosed entry garden is like a room because you can think about it as having the elements of a room in your home—walls, a ceiling and a floor. And you can fashion garden rooms in diverse ways to suit your style of living and to complement your home's architecture.

Walls for enclosure

My first task with clients is selecting the walls. Plants, fences or masonry can form a garden wall (see top photo, right) and each material has its own set of advantages and disadvantages. Plants offer the benefit of foliage and flowers or berries, depending on the specific varieties chosen, but they generally occupy more space than a fence or wall and require more upkeep. Plants often outreach their bounds, so they will need pruning. Still, the beauty of a living hedge or shrub border is appealing, especially if the homeowner has enough time for maintenance or can afford to hire help.

Hedges occupy less space than looser shrub borders, and they give a crisp, formal appearance to the garden. But for complete privacy, evergreens are a must. I prefer hedges made of needled evergreens—their fine texture creates just

the right backdrop for the showier border shrubs and perennials. Arborvitaes (*Thuja occidentalis*), yews (*Taxus baccata, Taxus × media*), incense cedars (*Calocedrus decurrens*) and Canadian hemlocks (*Tsuga canadensis*) are excellent choices in my Oregon climate.

I avoid plants with big shiny leaves because their glossiness will catch the eye and compete too much with flowering plants. English laurel and photinia not only suffer from this fault but also grow too quickly and require endless clipping. I recommend slower-growing plants that top out at the desired height and need only a little clipping. Broadleaved evergreen shrubs also provide screening without requiring frequent trimming. They also need less maintenance but occupy more space. Laurustinus (*Viburnum tinus*), with its medium-size leaves and white fall and winter flowers followed by blue berries, has year-round interest. Japanese holly (*Ilex crenata*) offers small, rounded green leaves, while English holly (*Ilex aquifolium*) has the distinction of larger spiny leaves, and berries on some varieties. I am partial to the variegated English hollies, especially silver-margined holly (*I. aquifolium* 'Argenteomarginata'), which is actually green edged with

Plantings in front of a fence or over a gate reinforce privacy. 'Glorie de Dijon' climbing rose, a cut-leaf Japanese maple, *Hosta sieboldii* and other plantings in front of this fence create walls that obscure the garden from the public's gaze.

Create special effects by using rough, uneven or irregular materials for the walls and floor of the enclosed entry. The floor and wall elements here are created with a Japanese-style fence and gate, and a stone floor.

cream. I like red clusterberry (*Cotoneaster lacteus*) for its graceful, arching shape and its cheerful bunches of red berries in late fall and winter. Strawberry tree (*Arbutus unedo*), a large shrub, intrigues me with its reddish brown bark and fall fruit that dangles like a cherry but has a strawberry's bumpy texture. In shade, the taller rhododendrons, camellias and andromedas (*Pieris japonica*) make fine screening shrubs, with the added attraction of showy spring flowers.

Fences and masonry walls are more expensive than plants but have two strong advantages—immediate privacy and lower maintenance. Walls made of wood, stone or brick add solidity to the garden and offer interesting contrast with the softer texture of the plants. The posts, rails, caps and latticework of wooden fences contribute rhythmic patterns to the garden. Stone and brick add their own unique colors and textures along with a feeling of age and permanence. All of these constructed walls are invitations to train climbing roses, honeysuckle, clematis and other vines. Because they offer some protection from wind and cold, walls create shelter for growing marginally hardy plants.

Ceilings for coziness

Although a garden room doesn't need a ceiling since the enclosed entry is close to the house, a canopy of some sort will help make a gradual transition from a looming building to the walls and plants of the garden. A tree canopy is a good choice for that purpose, and it will provide some shade at the same time. When I plan a garden, I make sure to place trees far enough from the house—at least half the distance of the canopy's ultimate spread—to allow their branches to grow freely.

Structures can also provide a ceiling for the entry garden (see photo, p. 8), preferably in a style that resembles the architecture of the home. A pergola can extend from the house and serve as a covered walkway. With trelliswork at the top, it can also support climbing plants and provide shade. A freestanding arbor toward the center of the entry garden can shade a seating area and be a focus of visual interest from inside the house. The same arbor placed closer to the front gate can function as a welcoming station for guests. I encourage my clients to construct built-in benches beneath arbors. The combined features of overhead flowering plants and shade below make an irresistible place to sit and relax. Of course, if the entry is small and sunny space is limited, I sometimes forgo any shade-producing canopy and let the sky be the ceiling (see photo, above).

With a well-placed bench, the garden becomes an outdoor room. Situated beneath an espaliered pomegranate, a bench allows admirers to sit and enjoy this garden rather than just pass it by on the way to the front door. A water garden enhanced by 'Caesar's Brother' Siberian iris makes for a tranquil view.

Floors for stability

The garden floor should be a strong, silent partner—there to keep your feet dry, your furniture steady and your plants looking beautiful. One of the loveliest gardens I've ever visited has a floor made of brick pavers. Brick curbs edge the beds to retain soil and set off paths. The pink-orange tones of brick add a rich color that contrasts with and complements plants. I like a brick garden floor when the house is also made of brick; it unifies home and garden.

Poured concrete is another permanent material that affords a firm, dry surface. Because plain concrete forms a glaring white surface, I prefer exposed aggregate or tinted concrete to tone it down. A muted-color concrete allows your flowers to shine, not your floor.

Stone makes a handsome entry surface, adding age and character to the garden (see bottom photo, p. 9). The surface of some stone floors is irregular, creating interest but making it less predictable underfoot. However, the color and texture of stone are hard to beat. I love planting fragrant plants, such as flowering thyme, cottage pinks and Corsican mint, in the crevices of stone floors. Treading on thyme and mint releases their scent, adding another dimension to the garden.

A less permanent material, such as crushed rock or fine gravel, can also surface the garden floor. Choose small (¼ in. or smaller) stones that will pack down firmly—larger gravel tends to slide underfoot. A curb or retaining edge can keep rock from creeping into the beds. Gravel and crushed rock need renewing from time to time, so they require more maintenance than poured concrete, stone or brick pavers. Another drawback is that weed seeds tend to germinate in floors made of crushed rock, but seedlings are easy enough to pull out. Actually, I think it's fun to leave occasional interesting self-sowers in the ground, à la John Brookes, the English garden designer who decorated his charming gravel paths with bold, gray-leaved mulleins (*Verbascum bombyciferum*).

Design to suit your taste

No matter which style you select for your entry garden, there are endless possibilities for creating walls, ceilings and floors. Use these design principles as a starting point. The entry to your home belongs to you, and it should be yours to enjoy in comfort and privacy. □

Barbara Ashmun, author of The Garden Design Primer, *is a landscape designer and teacher in Portland, Oregon.*

A Cozy Sitting Garden

Colorful plants and imaginative design make the most of a small area

A chair waits invitingly in the shade of a hawthorn tree in the author's garden. Nearby, a flower bed blazes with red nicotianas and wax begonias, yellow tuberous begonias and coreopsis. Tall umbrella plants cool their feet in a tiny pond. (Photo taken at A on site plan on p. 13.)

by Jerry Glick

I feel that every garden, regardless of size, needs an intimate spot for relaxing, reading a good book, enjoying colorful flowers or listening to the sound of water splash-ing in a pool. My backyard presented the perfect oppor-tunity to make such a spot. In the Columbus, Ohio, neigh-borhood where I live, the 19th century brick cottages sit close together on postage-stamp-sized lots—my backyard is just 30 ft. by 40 ft. So I had to figure out how to fit everything I wanted in a limited area. I hoped to create a private garden getaway—a place to rest body and soul that would be loaded with annuals and perennials for season-long color.

All photos: Jesse Cabungcal

A small, brick patio adds elbow room and a dining area to the postage-stamp garden. (Photo taken at B.)

I used several design techniques that work equally well in small or large gardens. With my approach, you could make a colorful sitting nook, a patio or deck garden, or a series of small gardens within a larger one. Here are my ideas for creating a sense of spaciousness, framing views, adding height to the garden, establishing resting places and growing flowering plants for all-season color.

Creating a sense of spaciousness

When I moved in, my tiny yard was overgrown with ivy, shrubs and trees. I created the illusion of spaciousness by making open areas—a deck and a patio—and ringing them with flower beds. Dividing the garden into several small, distinct areas also makes it seem bigger.

In such a small garden, or in small areas within a larger garden, it is especially important to leave some space open to prevent a cluttered look and to lead the eye through the design. I cleared away all the trees except a weeping cherry, a crabapple and a hawthorn, and I pruned them to a size in keeping with the small yard. Paths between the beds keep the plants from running together in an untidy jumble and lead people through the garden (see site plan on p. 13). A brick patio gives me and my guests some elbow room.

The materials I chose for paving and for a fence are unobtrusive, matching the house and a carriage house at the back of the property. The patio, which sits behind the brick house, is made of salvaged brick. A low deck of weathered wood surrounds a little pond, and a boardwalk runs along the back of the garden, blending in with the wooden fence and wood siding of the carriage house.

Hinting at more to come—To increase the sense of spaciousness, I also used a few optical tricks when I laid out my garden. Placing plants or objects so they must be walked around to see what's beyond creates mystery and suggests there is more garden just out of sight. Visitors then anticipate whatever lies on the other side. To give this impression, I surrounded the deck and patio with planting beds and paths laid out at angles that force people to walk around each one to see the next. To partially screen some areas of the garden from others, I planted tall plants such as butterfly bush (*Buddleia davidii* 'Black Knight'), a summer-blooming, woody shrub, in the beds and umbrella plant (*Cyperus alternifolius*) in the pond (see photo on p. 11).

Adding privacy and height

I wanted a tranquil garden oasis; with neighbors on both sides, I had to make it private. So I surrounded the garden

Yellow-flowered heliopsis and lavender butterfly bush tower over pink bleeding-hearts, pink begonias, yellow coreopsis and pink verbena. (Photo taken at C.)

with a 6-ft. tall wooden fence. The fence effectively screens out my neighbors and frames the garden, focusing attention within. The fence is high enough to form a background for the tall plants in the garden. It's also a foil for the large hanging baskets suspended from the trees, and for half-baskets loaded with colorful annuals attached to it. The fence, tall plants and hanging baskets all draw the eye upward, vertically increasing the apparent size of the garden.

Places to rest the body and soul

With so many plants in a garden, the eye needs a few large, simple shapes to contemplate; the body needs a shady spot in which to sit and listen to restful sounds. My fish pond, complete with water plants and a small, cascading waterfall, is only a couple of feet in diameter—in keeping with the overall proportions of the garden—but the soothing sound of running water and the glint of goldfish beneath its surface offer immense rewards. It is situated nearly in the center of everything. Next to the pond, a white canvas chair draws me like a beacon to the shade of the hawthorn tree, where I can sit and survey the entire garden. On the patio, a white umbrella-table and chairs offer another shady spot to sit.

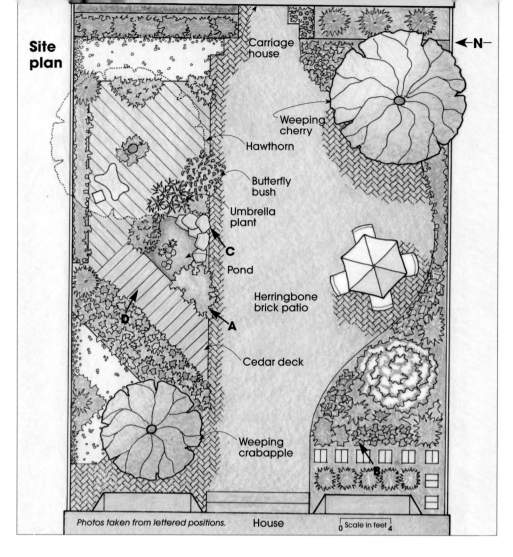

Site plan

Carriage house

N

Weeping cherry

Hawthorn

Butterfly bush

Umbrella plant

C

Pond

Herringbone brick patio

A

Cedar deck

B

Weeping crabapple

D

Photos taken from lettered positions.

House

Scale in feet
0   4

A hawthorn tree and a weeping cherry partially disguise the facade of an old carriage house and add vertical scale to the author's backyard sitting garden. (Photo taken at D.)

Splashes of color all season

I pack my flowers together cottage-garden fashion in an exuberant mix of colors and textures that overlap and spill onto the paving. I use a combination of annuals and perennials in a variety of heights and leaf textures. My garden is small, however, so I don't have the luxury of planting indiscriminately. I select my plants for overlapping bloom periods and bright flower colors. I also use container plants in full bloom to replace bloomed-out specimens and to spike beds of ivy with color. I think it's fun to use potted plants that are not typically grown outdoors in summer in the Midwest—tropical hibiscus, oleander and bougainvillea. They flower all summer in shades ranging from hot pink and lavender to the brightest scarlet. I overwinter these potted plants indoors.

In order to make my limited-size garden interesting, functional and private, I let my wishes overcome conventional wisdom, which suggests that it takes a big area to have a great garden. I say that it just takes some imagination, lots of plants and a few design tricks. Last summer I managed to keep annuals in full color late into the season, when they join the mums in a crescendo of color.

My little garden lets me block out the hubbub of city life. Here I enter a world of nature where I watch squirrels, birds and butterflies. Last summer I had garden visitors daily; their enjoyment plus my own was reward enough. ∎

Jerry Glick's garden is in the historic German Village neighborhood of Columbus, Ohio.

Illustration: Vince Babak

Viewed from the upper deck outside the author's house, a partially enclosed dining patio in the distance beckons. Dividing the garden into separate areas provides places for relaxing alone or entertaining friends and makes a small yard seem more spacious.

An Intimate Garden for Entertaining

Levels and nooks make a quiet haven

by Steve Kiely

When I moved into my 1920's cottage six years ago, it had a small, narrow backyard that overlooked the neighbors' yards and was exposed to a noisy street. The yard was a patch of broken concrete, weeds and untrimmed shrubs and trees. Light conditions also were extreme, ranging from deep shade to searing afternoon sun.

Yet I wanted a garden here, a garden with a tranquil, intimate and comfortable atmosphere, a place where I could be equally comfortable alone or with friends. At the same time I wanted the yard to feel more spacious than it actually was. Since my house is also small, I hoped the garden would serve as an outdoor extension of it. And the garden would have to be low-maintenance—I have a full-time job, and I wanted to spend the majority of my

All photos: except where noted, Nancy Beaubaire

The author enjoys his morning coffee in a gazebo on the upper deck. The awnings on the roof and walls unroll individually to protect this outdoor room from sun, wind, rain and snow. The gazebo is ringed with potted plants such as blue agapanthus and vine maple.

time in the garden reading, meditating and relaxing, not mowing, weeding and watering. Finally, I hoped to use the garden year-round—on a clear, winter day here in Denver, Colorado, the temperature can be a balmy 60°F.

Back then I was a novice at gardening, having grown nothing more than geraniums and marigolds where I lived previously. And because this hobby was new to me, I wanted a chance to observe plants and to experiment with them. I began by growing common plants you can buy at the supermarket and gradually introduced more unusual ones (see "Everyday plants" on p. 17).

Today, my garden offers welcome respite from the clamor of city living. In solitude, it offers me a quiet haven; filled with friends, it encourages camaraderie. A deck and multiple levels of patios provide room-like areas for entertaining, dining and relaxing. An 8-ft. tall wooden fence provides privacy and security. Raised landscape-tie planting beds of various heights and shapes frame the "rooms" and display

a host of small and medium-sized, easy-care plants. Clay pots teeming with flowers and vines add splashes of color throughout the garden.

Creating an intimate ambience

The yard had a gentle slope, so I decided to carve out different levels, ultimately ending up with three patios and a deck. Each area is unique, and I gravitate from one to another, depending on the time of day and what I want to do. Sometimes I'm pulled to a part of the garden warmed by the sun; other times I'm drawn to an area bursting with flowers just because of my need to get lost among them.

A nook with a view—The first room in the garden is a large, raised wooden deck, 14 ft. × 31 ft., that extends from the upper level of the house over a garage (see photo on p. 16). From the deck, I can take in a grand view of almost all of the garden. A wide staircase down to the main level ties the deck in with the other patios. The centerpiece of the deck is an 8 ft. ×

9 ft. gazebo made of cedar lattice, just big enough to comfortably seat four people around a large coffee table (see photo above). Individual awnings can be unrolled like window shades to cover the walls and roof, offering varying degrees of privacy and protection from the elements.

Merely a step out from an upstairs bedroom, the gazebo functions as a true extension of the house. In the early morning hours, it's my favorite place to enjoy coffee and a newspaper. I love to sit in the gazebo with the roof awning shut, watching and smelling the dramatic summer storms that frequently roll in from the mountains. I also enjoy pulling back the awnings to admire colorful sunsets and starry nighttime skies.

Big barrels of shrubs and flowers surround the gazebo, making it a cozy conversation nook as well as a soothing place to be alone. Closer to the house, where the deck is partially shaded by a large chokecherry tree, I've planted mostly pastel flowers and silver-leaved plants, spiced up with the tubular, salmon flowers of *Fuchsia* 'Gardenmeister Bohnstedt', an annual that blooms all summer. In the sunnier areas around the gazebo, I like hot colors—a raucous mix of yellow, red and bright pink zinnias, red and yellow Asiatic lilies, and yellow dahlberg daisies. For the winter interest of its branched, brown stems, I planted a lovely broom, *Cytisus scoparius* 'Moonlight'. This deciduous small shrub is dotted with buttery yellow flowers in spring.

A private cubbyhole—At the foot of the stairs leading down from the upper deck, there is a very secluded patio, just 8 ft. × 13 ft., tucked under the chokecherry tree. I like cubbyholes like this—places where I can get lost and no one sees me. Paved with dry-laid stones I gathered from the mountains, this private patio has become my favorite place for reading and meditating.

This area is rather heavily shaded, so I planted it mainly with pastel-flowered impatiens, cascading blue and white lobelia, purple and white violets, and cool, luscious mosses. At night, the silver-edged ground cover lamium 'White Nancy' reflects moonlight and garden lights, guiding my steps and adding a luminous glow.

Just a few feet away is a four-tiered fountain. The sound of its gentle, trickling flow masks traffic noises while providing a beautiful, tranquil setting. It is amazing to sit quietly in the early morning sun and watch the birds, squirrels and neighborhood cats that visit the fountain to drink and bathe.

An outdoor dining room—At the far end of the yard I built a 12 ft. × 15 ft. wood patio under the shade of a spruce tree, which provides protection from the weather (see photo on p. 14). Landscape-tie planters on both sides of the entry create a doorway of sorts. They make the patio feel like an enclosed room; so does the tall wooden fence on two sides. Two steps descending into the patio emphasize that it's a distinct space, as does the change in materials from the stone path leading to the patio to the stone and brick steps.

From the patio you can see the fountain and catch glimpses of the upper deck, but otherwise it's quite secluded. An umbrella-covered table and wicker chairs make this area the perfect place for evening dining. In such an intimate setting, conversation flows freely.

The landscape-tie planters surrounding the patio are 2 ft. wide and range from 1 ft. to 5 ft. tall. They over-

flow with plants to delight the nose and palate. Fragrant night-scented stock, nicotiana and scented geraniums perfume the air, creating a heavenly atmosphere. Interspersed among them are herbs, such as parsley, thyme, chives and rosemary, which I pick fresh to add to meals, a simple feat that certainly impresses my guests.

To partially hide the patio from view, I made the planter on one side of the entry taller than the one on the other and included small shrubs in it that fit the scale of the garden and add winter interest. I chose plants that stand out against snow. There's a splash of burgundy from the leaves of a dwarf

Japanese barberry, a base of green from low-growing evergreens, and accents of red from a cotoneaster's berries. The hazelnut, 'Harry Lauder's Walking Stick' (*Corylus avellana* 'Contorta') completes the winter picture with its gnarled, twisted branches.

In summer, miniature hollyhocks and Asiatic lilies add some height without making a dense screen. The silvery leaves of Japanese painted ferns (*Athyrium goeringianum* 'Pictum') reflect light at night, while the deep purple foliage of the perennial heuchera 'Palace Purple' contrasts nicely with the white flowers of nicotiana and stock during the day.

A surprise around the corner—Hidden beneath the upper deck is a truly whimsical patio. Once a carport, this rectangular concrete slab afforded a view only of a plain fence; it was utterly barren. For fun I've recreated the panoramic view I often enjoy from a nearby city park that overlooks downtown Denver and the majestic Rocky Mountains. I built a 6-ft. wide raised bed along the length of the fence, and positioned cedar posts upright in the bed to represent several of the downtown skyscrapers. For the background, I made mountain peaks from strips of redwood nailed to

A view from the outdoor dining area takes in the stairs to the upper deck and gazebo. Small shrubs and perennials in the foreground hide the entry to a secret patio beneath the deck. Beyond the stairs lies a tiny patio shaded by a chokecherry tree.

the fence. Dwarf Alberta spruces planted in the foreground and various ground covers interspersed between the "buildings" create a park-like setting. A miniature stone pathway winds through this diorama, creating an illusion of distance. Pots filled with coleus and impatiens add color.

One of the most enjoyable aspects of this patio is that it's mostly hidden. Visitors catch only a glimpse of it through lath beneath the stairs near the chokecherry and are enticed to figure out how to enter it. From the lower dining patio, you can see only the entrance to this hidden patio, a tantalizing hint of something beyond.

Making a yard seem bigger

It might sound as though I have crammed too much into a very small yard, but several techniques make the garden appear much larger than it is. Try them if you want a more spacious-looking yard.

• Creating different levels and room-like areas encourages people to immerse themselves in each distinct environment, rather than focus on the small size of the whole yard. Even a slight change in level creates the illusion of a larger area.

• Varying the size and heights of planting beds breaks the movement of your eyes as you stop and study each bed. This adds dimension to the landscape and offers points of interest.

By building up some of the beds to eye level and planting them with small and medium-sized plants in scale with a small garden, I created the impression of a larger, more mature garden. Vines and cascading plants tumble over the edges of the beds, adding fullness without taking up much space.

• Enticing viewers with stairs and paths draws them from one area to another, encouraging full exploration of the garden and creating the impression of a larger area. But because I've used paving materials that look and feel irregular, such as the used brick and uneven stones that form my paths, visitors walk slowly and savor their surroundings. Interplanting the paving with creeping thyme, which releases wonderful scents when trod upon, causes people to linger even more.

Stairs and paths also leave visitors wondering what lies ahead, just out of sight. When people don't see a defined area, they often imagine a larger one. In my garden, several miniature paths meandering through the planting beds lead nowhere, but they take the eye and the mind on a journey.

• Establishing several sitting areas from which the garden can be viewed gives you a chance to see many gardens in one. No matter which direction you look, there can be something to catch your eye. My favorite location for viewing is the tiny patio beside the water fountain. From there I can see all the other areas only partially, so I'm soon up and roaming again. □

Steve Kiely enjoys his garden year-round in Denver, Colorado.

Photo: Rob Proctor; illustration, Grace Schaar

Everyday plants

Ordinary plants nestle together in containers to create a splash of color all summer. Mostly annuals, all are available at garden centers and grocery store nurseries.

Key to photo above

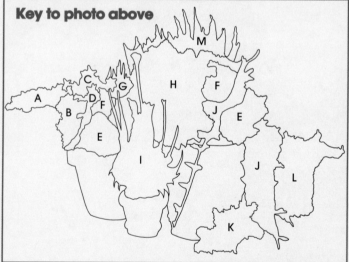

A - Calendula
B - Dianthus
C - Nicotiana
D - Dusty miller
E - Lobelia
F - Perilla
G - Iris
H - Petunia
I - Curry plant
J - Vinca
K - Johnny-jump-ups
L - Marigolds
M - Salvia

When I began this garden, I didn't know an annual from a perennial. I bought common plants from the grocery store at bargain prices, happy with the standard fare of marigolds, geraniums and petunias. You'd be amazed at the magic you can create with ordinary plants. Most of those I started with are annuals that bloom their colorful heads off for a long time.

These plants can keep you satisfied for a long time, perhaps forever. Or, like me, you might decide to expand your repertoire. Indeed, exploring the world of plants has been the most fulfilling aspect of my garden. Now I find winners by trial and error. In fact, I feel that if I haven't killed at least ten plants a year, I'm not pushing myself enough.

But don't think I've forgotten the grocery store plants that gave me the encouragement to garden in the first place. I still delight in buying a 59-cent pack of begonias, and the sight and smell of a petunia will always have a place in my garden. —S.K.

The orange calendula 'Mandarin' is backed by the yellow-centered dahlia 'Little Red Riding Hood' and golden yarrow, with a dollop of purple salvia 'Victoria' for contrast. Hot-colored flowers make a garden jump to life.

In the author's enclosed garden, hot-colored flowers in vivid reds, oranges and yellows freely co-mingle.

A Home for Hot Colors

Red, yellow and orange flowers
spice up a garden of their own

by Elisabeth Sheldon

For many years I have tended a long mixed border consisting mostly of perennials. Its pastels of pink, lavender, lemon yellow, blue, gray and white, punctuated with an occasional touch of crimson, reflect the dominant colors of the perennial flowers that survive in my New York State garden

in USDA Hardiness Zone 5 (-20°F.) They are cool colors, peaceful and serene. At times I tried to include hot colors—strong, brassy yellows, oranges, scarlets or vermilions—but I found they disturbed the harmony of the border. I thus banished the deep yellow yarrows, black-eyed Susans, false sunflowers and other strident individuals to the far reaches of my temporary beds. I didn't throw them on the compost heap, you will notice; I merely isolated the hot-colored flowers, keeping them until I would find a way to

use them effectively. Meanwhile I trotted out to visit them occasionally when I needed a pick-me-up.

Now, I have loved (and still love) my long, pastel border, but with the passage of years I began to long for stronger stuff. I began to think of ways to use intense colors where they wouldn't interfere with the cool border symphony. I considered several sites before I finally decided to enclose part of my old plant nursery, at one end of the pastel border and adjacent to my woods garden, and make it into

In fall, the flowers of *Helenium autumnale* 'Bruno', a perennial, blanket 2-ft. to 4-ft. tall stems.

a garden of hot colors. It was a particularly good spot for the new garden, because visitors would walk along the long, cool border, then suddenly be knocked flat when they encountered the explosion of color.

The border and new garden look very different. My informal perennial border of pastels is designed with a series of curves on the front edge played against a long, straight line behind. Since the new garden would be inside a smallish rectangular area (about 20 ft. × 30 ft.), I felt it required a formal plan with no curves. A narrow central path begins at the gate, bisects three paved rectangles and ends with a bench. It's a very stiff and formal outline, compensated for by the exuberance of the planting.

It would have been nice to enclose the garden with a tall, clipped hedge, but the space was too small. Nor did I want to wait for shrubs to grow or to spend a lot of time shearing them. I thus opted for a plain, 5-ft. tall cedar fence. By the time the fence was up and I had laid the paving and planted the garden, I had a secret jungle retreat. And there I go, at least once a day, to sit, to drink in the color combinations and to bring myself to a mild state of innocent intoxication.

Flame red campion 'Vesuvius' sizzles for several weeks in summer next to black-eyed Susan 'Marmalade'.

Design principles for hot-colored flowers

In designing and planting this garden, I have developed four principles that can be applied to other bold gardens.

Isolate hot colors—Because hot colors are so visually stimulating (and hard to combine with other colors), I think they should be separated from the rest of the garden. Besides, if you look at them every time you walk outdoors, they're apt to lose their impact. Because the area I chose for my hot-color garden is so flat, I had to enclose it to keep it distinct (see photo on p. 19). Gardeners with more uneven territory

could separate hot colors by putting them on one side of a knoll, declivity or terrace. Or they could place them in back of a hedge or on the far side of a building.

Choose complementary building materials—A building or fence behind the planting should be of a color that will enhance the flower colors, not detract from them. The gray of cedar fencing seems perfect (see photo on p. 21), but white could be even more dramatic. Brown wood might be harmonious, but would create a heavier effect than gray or white. Avoid by all means pink, red, yellow or bright green backgrounds. (The green of a hedge, which can serve as a perfectly suitable backdrop, is quite different from most greens that come out of a can.) Pink, red or yellow would cause flowers of related colors to lose importance. For the paving, the gray-maroon of paving bricks, which I used, is generally harmonious. Weathered brick would also work well. Gray flagstone would have been a fine color, but hard to fit into the small, geometric shapes of my paved area.

Photos: above, Susan Kahn; below, Dency Kane

Repeat colors and shapes—When I planned the planting, I remembered that in gardening as in painting, repetition of color and form is absolutely necessary for harmony and unity. You don't have to use the same plant over and over, but you should find plants of the same shape and/or flower color that bloom at the same time. For example, the orange of calendulas is repeated by marigolds. Red and gold gaillardias echo the red and gold of dahlias. The color repeats, though the plants do not.

I first thought of making symmetrical plantings in the new formal garden, one side as a mirror image of the other. That seemed so boring that I decided, instead, to try to balance the two sides using similar colors and forms. Tall red and gold heleniums (*Helenium autumnale* cvs.) grow on both sides of the garden but are not necessarily opposite one another. *Dahlia* 'Bishop of Llandaff' stands against one fence, *Dahlia* 'Tasagore' against the other. Both have the most beautiful purple foliage and what British plantsman Graham Stuart Thomas calls "fierce" red flowers. I placed different varieties of red daylilies on each side.

Some plantings are symmetrical, though. Yellow coreopsis (*Coreopsis auriculata* 'Nana'), 1 ft. tall, sits on each of the four corners of the garden. Orange 'Enchantment' lilies stand with dark purple Japanese iris in the two far corners. Short 'Disco Red' marigolds edge opposite sides of the paths; I've paired 'Disco Orange' marigolds similarly. They hold their jewel-like, flat, single flowers tight against low, dark green, incised foliage and seem to never stop flowering. These are the only examples of perfect symmetry.

Be bold—Choosing flowers for a hot-color garden involves a certain amount of experimentation and a willingness—at least in my case—to discard a few long-cherished prejudices. In our climate, a gardener has to go tropical and look for annuals and bulb plants to get a volcanic display. But I have always despised marigolds, cannas, dahlias and gladiolus. Going in for "proper" perennials as I did, I was above such frivolous individuals. For my sins, I'm now having to recant as I glory in their startling colors.

Favorite hot-colored flowers
I began my new garden with hot-colored perennials I already had in reserve: yarrows (*Achillea* 'Gold Plate'

Orange Mexican sunflower and golden yarrow tower over reddish-orange cosmos, yellow coreopsis and red dahlias in the author's garden.

The true orange of 'Enchantment' lilies, an unusual color for a hardy perennial, appears even more vibrant paired with the purple spikes of salvia 'Victoria'.

and *A.* 'Coronation Gold') and red and yellow heleniums (see photo at the top of p. 20). I also planted two tall sunflower relatives with double yellow poufs for flowers—*Heliopsis scabra* 'Golden Plume' and *Helianthus* × *multiflorus* 'Flore-plena', which proved too big, and which I later evicted—adding red and purple bee balms (*Monarda* spp.), yellow coreopsis, and red and yellow daylilies.

Then I started plowing through catalogs looking for more hot-colored flowers. I've made some wonderful discov-

Photos: above, Mark Kane; below, Dency Kane

eries. The tender perennial campion (Lychnis × arkwrightii 'Vesuvius') provides one of the most intense flame reds available, on 18-in. plants distinguished by rich maroon foliage (see photo on p. 20). It blooms for several weeks and is kind enough to seed itself about every year.

Breeders have doubled the number of flower petals of the annual blanketflower (Gaillardia pulchella 'Red Plume', see photo at right) to the point where it no longer looks like a gaillardia—a procedure which I am on record as vigorously opposing. But, since it produces an endless supply of chianti-red flowers on 1½-ft. tall plants, I must shame-facedly admit to being grateful for it. I use the perennial Gaillardia × grandiflora 'Burgundy' with no shame, since it has a single row of deep red petals.

For me, dark purple—either the true purple of some flowers or the "purple" (actually dark wine, maroon or blackish red) of leaves—is the best companion to the warmer hues. Along with the dahlias 'Bishop of Llandaff' (which, to my knowledge, is unavailable in the U.S.) and 'Tasagore', I've planted 'Japanese Bishop', all for their purple foliage. Their leaves echo those of Chinese basil (Perilla frutescens) and basil (Ocimum basilicum 'Purple Ruffles'). Both are easy-to-grow annuals that I've planted throughout the garden. Perilla loses its lovely color when it goes to seed and must be discarded, but 'Purple Ruffles' basil remains attractive all summer. The tender sweet-potato vine (Ipomoea batatas 'Blackie') has the darkest foliage of all, with near-black, deeply lobed leaves.

My garden is full of red, yellow and orange, especially in July. 'Sunny Red' cosmos, an annual, isn't really red but a pretty reddish-orange. It blooms for several weeks. Pure orange is found in 'Mandarin' calendulas (see photo on p. 18), in some of the daylilies and especially in 'Enchantment' lilies (see photo on p. 21). The 4-ft. Mexican sunflower (Tithonia rotundifolia), an annual, has velvety leaves and large, soft orange (another orange!) daisies. It shows well against the big purple flowers of Clematis × jackmanii on the fence. There is also an orange-gold swath of the annual black-eyed Susan (Rudbeckia hirta 'Marmalade'), bold

The dark red blossoms of the annual blanketflower 'Red Plume' cap 1½-ft. tall plants all summer. Annuals can provide bolder colors and longer bloom times than most perennials can.

SOURCES

Most of the perennials mentioned in this article are available from local retail or mail-order nurseries. The following nurseries sell a wide range of hot-colored annuals:

Seeds:

Park Seed Co., Cokesbury Road, Greenwood, SC 29647-0001; 800-845-3369. Catalog free.

Stokes Seeds, Inc., P.O. Box 548, Buffalo, NY 14240; 800-263-7233. Catalog free.

Thompson & Morgan, Inc., P.O. Box 1308, Jackson, NJ 08527; 201-363-2225. Catalog free.

Dahlias, other tubers or bulbs:

Dutch Gardens, Inc., P.O. Box 200, Adelphia, NJ 07710; 908-780-2713. Catalog free.

Swan Island Dahlias, P.O. Box 700, Canby, OR 97013; 503-266-7711. Catalog $3.

and brassy (see photo on p. 20). Both it and the Mexican sunflower seem to bloom forever.

When purple Japanese iris fade, they are followed by the purple spikes of annual salvia (Salvia farinacea 'Victoria'). Short, fat mounds of dahlia 'Little Red Riding Hood' have single red flowers with yellow centers, set off by purple bee balms and 15-in. tall blue spikes of veronica (Veronica spicata 'Blue Fox'). There's lots of gold yarrow, lots of red and yellow daylilies and behind them, proper lilies (Lilium 'Gran

Paradiso' and 'Barcellona'). They make outfacing cartwheels of orange, scarlet and dark red.

Coreopsis (Coreopsis verticillata 'Zagreb') is pretty with its sheets of small, yellow ray flowers and feathery foliage. Not smashing but nice. More striking are the blossoms, deep yellow and brown, of the annual chrysanthemum (Chrysanthemum carinatum 'Zebra'). The vermilion knobs of globe amaranth (Gomphrena hybrida 'Strawberry Fayre', an excellent flower for drying sold in some catalogs as 'Strawberry Fields') bloom on eternally through summer and fall until a hard frost. These flowers never seem to fade, flop or drop. Apparently they're as everlasting in life as in death.

You may have been appalled by this account, or you may have been inspired to plant your own garden of hot colors. If so, you'll have to search for plants that will thrive in your environment. If you garden in the South or on the West Coast, you might have the advantage in this regard—the growing season is longer, and you needn't lift so many bulbs and tubers for overwintering indoors. The combination of heat and humidity in the South, however, might rule out some plants I can grow here in New York.

When you've chosen your plants, you can begin to combine them in ways that suit you. You may want to include bright pinks or temper the atmosphere with whites or blues or silver instead of the dark purple flowers or foliage I prefer, but that's only personal taste. Last summer I thought to rest the eye with grays and whites as well as purples. I tried gray, felt-leaved helichrysums, which are not hardy here, in pots. I also planted a senecio (Senecio leucostachys) against the back wall. This striking perennial bears bright silver, finely cut foliage. I think the helichrysums were a mistake—they looked irrelevant or as if they were all dressed up and had come to the wrong party. But there are so many other possibilities. Are you intrigued? Then I encourage you to get out the catalogues and start planning. □

Elisabeth Sheldon is a gardener, writer and lecturer who lives in Lansing, New York. She wrote A Proper Garden *(Stackpole Books, 1989).*

The regal purple of the clematis on the fence and of the iris in the foreground is a foil for the brassy gold of a long-blooming, annual black-eyed Susan. Hot colors like these wake up any garden visitor.

Photo: Dency Kane

A Front-Yard Retreat

Artful design fashions a private patio

In a small front yard, concrete pads outlined with brick lead to the courtyard designed and built by the author. The stone wall shelters a patio and fountain without looking like a blank fortress.

by Chris D. Moore

On a small property, the front yard is precious. Usually it's gardened for show and not for use, because there's too little room to do both. In my small front yard, however, I've managed to build a patio *and* make a welcoming landscape. I walled in the patio without making a fortress that would shun the neighborhood. Windows in the wall, a broad path to the front gate and perennial flowers make the front yard inviting. Hidden behind the wall, a fountain and intimate plantings offer a cool refuge.

When my wife, Jan, and I went looking for a larger home back in 1987, this one looked lackluster from the street. But we liked the neighborhood, the interior was perfect, and we decided we could remedy the facade with landscaping.

Shortly after we moved in, I began "playing" with the 50-ft. × 100-ft. lot on paper. Since we enjoy having meals outdoors, we wanted some part of the property devoted to an area for sitting and relaxing. And since we planned to eventually add on to the house in the back, it seemed best to create a private area in front. Also, despite the street noise, the front yard is more pleasant than the back in the heat of the day because it faces north. In our previous house, we had built a partially fenced courtyard and entry that featured a fish pond, waterfall, and some lush landscaping. I decided to do something similar here.

Water and stonework

There were two elements I wanted to incorporate in the design: stone and the sound of water. In my work as a landscape architect, I have come to view the sound of water as a necessity. It adds a note of serenity that's difficult to duplicate any other way, while masking intrusive noises from the street. Stone is a common building material in our neighborhood. The local building stone—called engineer's rock—has attractive light earth tones and grays, and it's plentiful and relatively inexpensive.

I decided to build a brick patio in front of the house and surround it with a stone wall. The brick from the existing steps to the house inspired the choice of paving. The wall layout was dictated by the 20-ft. setback required by the city. Because the street runs at an angle to the house, I had to jog the wall (see the site plan on p. 26).

I wanted a wall, but I didn't want a fortress. I included three features that seem to shrink the mass of stone: I set the height at 5 ft. (without sacrificing privacy), I incorporated three grid-filled windows, and then, on the street side, I designed a planter with a knee-high stone wall on three sides. Because it steps down to the low wall, the high wall seems less massive. Crape myrtles in the 18-in. high planter also make the front yard more neighborly; they offer inter-

Water spouts from one of three concrete lion heads, the plumbing concealed in the stone wall. Water plants thrive in the pool, which is built of wood and fiberglass.

esting bark in winter and white flowers in summer.

I decided to install a narrow reflecting pool and fountain along the inside of the front wall. The location makes the fountain visible from the house. And the long, narrow shape of the reflecting pool minimizes the area it takes from the patio and maximizes the sound of the falling water. Three concrete lion's heads set into the wall jet water into the pool.

Lights

Lighting also played a key role in the design. I'd never used low voltage lights before, so I was anxious to experiment with some of the newer products on the market. While low voltage lights, in my experience, have limitations in large projects, for a project of this size, they work beautifully. These lights are simple to install, don't require an electrician, and the cable can be buried, instead of being installed in conduit.

Many people are familiar with the hardware store

A narrow pool runs along the front wall, and plants in pots provide accents of color. The twisting-steel gate was a gift made by the author's boss, Jack Chandler, a sculptor and landscape architect.

package of mushroom lights, but there are more options available. It takes a little research at a good lighting showroom to discover the wide range of fixtures for low voltage systems, but it's time well spent.

I chose canisters which shine upward, concealed in the raised planter, to highlight the crape myrtles and illuminate the outside of the wall for street side viewing. Inside the courtyard, I placed a floodlight on the wall, a narrow-focus spotlight on a garden statue, and a special underwater unit in the fountain. I also used custom wood garden lights of our firm's design along the entry path (see photo at right).

The entry path

The final element of the design was the path from the courtyard to the street. I feel strongly that pedestrians should be given their own path, instead of having to walk on the driveway to get to the front door. I decided to remove half the driveway to make room for the path and for more plants.

I designed a series of concrete rectangles edged with the same brick used in the patio for the path. I placed the rectangles alternately crosswise and lengthwise to create planting spaces and keep the path from marching parallel with the driveway. A ground cover of blue star creeper (*Laurentia fluviatilis*, sometimes listed as *Isotoma fluviatilis*), fills the 6-in. spaces between the pads. Other perennials and ornamental grasses provide additional color and foliage texture. The wooden lights illuminate them at night.

I never drew up a formal planting plan. Instead, I located sites for trees, lawn area and shrub beds, and selected plants later, at planting time, based on their availability and how they suited the landscape.

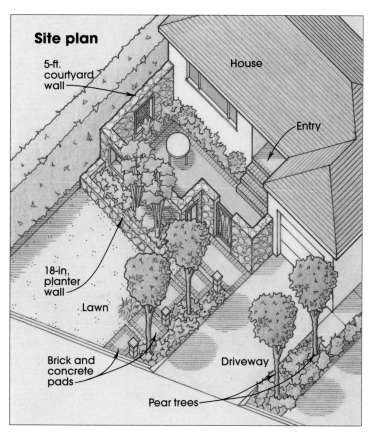

Site plan

5-ft. courtyard wall

House

Entry

18-in. planter wall

Lawn

Brick and concrete pads

Driveway

Pear trees

A wooden lighting fixture designed by the author's company illuminates the walk to the courtyard. By alternating the paving rectangles crosswise and lengthwise and leaving gaps between them, the author created spaces for plantings.

Construction

My wife and I did virtually all the construction. We started by saw-cutting and removing half the driveway and digging the retaining wall footings. We broke the concrete driveway remnants into chunks and recycled them into the 1-ft. footings for the wall. I put steel in the footings and preplumbed the electrical, irrigation and fountain systems before the start of wall construction.

The stone we used was left over from a job our firm had previously completed, and I borrowed a truck, hauled the stone over and dumped it in the front yard. I also constructed the wooden grid "windows" so they could be installed as the walls went up.

I hired a crew of masons to build the wall because I felt uncomfortable attempting it myself. They started laying up rock under my direction, and I worked with them to safeguard all the plumbing and to insure that the windows went in according to plan. As the walls reached toward 5 ft., I sensed that many of the neighbors had some serious reservations about the design and were wondering just what these new folks on the block might be up to.

Once the walls were completed, we excavated soil from the courtyard for the reflecting pool. Because I wanted the trough to be outfitted with ball valves, suction, overflow and drain to control water flow through the lions' heads, I knew I couldn't use a plastic liner. Concrete was too expensive, so I decided to use fiberglass. I built a frame of pressure-treated lumber, then fiberglassed over it and painted the surface black. I had never worked with fiberglass before, but found it an easy material to use.

A filter and pump for the fountain came from a pool contractor friend who

Illustration: Vince Babak

A raised planter filled with crape myrtles makes the stone wall around the courtyard in front of the house seem less imposing and more neighborly. A window and an airy gate also lessen the mass of the wall. Concrete ducks and a collection of potted plants greet visitors.

had removed them from a pool that was being upgraded. I installed the pump around the corner of the house, so its hum does not mask the sound of water from the fountain.

Once the pool was in place, we poured a concrete slab in the courtyard. Then we laid a course of bricks around the slab and filled in with bricks laid butt-to-butt on a ½-in. mortar setting bed.

The pads for the path are four inches deep, reinforced with wire mesh. I made the wood forms so the concrete had a ledge around the perimeter for the brick edging.

After we finished the wall, path and patio, we turned to the irrigation and electrical systems, and finally to planting. I dug sprinkler trenches, laid pipes and wiring, and installed sprinkler heads and lights. We amended the soil in the lawn area and laid down sod. Then I planted the rest of the yard in perennials.

Colorful Iceland poppies in pots brighten corners of the courtyard, adding to the limited planting spaces around two sides of the patio.

We wanted to have color for as much of the year as possible, but the available planting areas are small and narrow, so I chose small or dwarf cultivars. We also added spring-flowering bulbs to replace those torn up in construction.

It wasn't until the garden was planted that our neighbors began to admit their initial hesitations about the design. I think many had been afraid that we were walling them out rather than creating a more pleasing environment for all. The courtyard's northerly orientation makes it a wonderful place to eat lunch or dinner on a hot summer's day. The sound of water draws us to the courtyard almost daily. And the neighbors have adopted our yard for visiting, playing, and relaxing. □

Chris D. Moore is a landscape architect with Jack Chandler and Associates, a practice in the Napa, California, region.

A Classic Courtyard

Formal design brings the Italian Riviera to an urban space

by Marilyn K. Johnston

When my husband, Steve, and I got married, we quit our jobs, sold everything, and bought one-way tickets to Europe. We traveled for 18 months, residing for eight of them in Pavia, a small, medieval town in Italy, halfway between Milan and Genoa.

Near Pavia is Montalto Pavese, a 16th-century castle that has never left our memories. The castle has a formal garden made of clipped hedges, gravel paths and a topiary overlooking the Po River Valley and the Ligurian Apennines beyond. It is one of the most peaceful places I have ever been. When Steve and I returned to San Francisco and had the opportunity to create our own garden, there was never any doubt about what we would do: We would make a formal Italian Renaissance garden, filled with plants native to both Northern Italy and Northern California, to remind us of this magical place.

Our house in San Francisco is an 1883 Victorian. When we moved in nearly four years ago, the back yard was truly a blank slate. Behind the two-story, fully detached house, there was nothing but 1,500 square feet of concrete paving, a three-car garage and a tumble-down fence. There was not one square inch of dirt in which to plant. Although we were initially disappointed, we found the lack of landscaping gave us the freedom to create our own garden.

Elements of a formal garden

Our Italian Renaissance garden has certain typical formal elements, which include an orchard of espaliered fruit trees, geometric planting beds called parterres, fountains and an untamed area, or *bosco*. Important concepts in the garden are the axial relationships

A modern version of an Italian Renaissance courtyard, the author's garden includes traditional elements like geometric beds, paths and a fountain in the center. *(Photo taken at **A** on site plan, p. 30.)*

Before: The complete lack of landscaping gave the Johnstons plenty of freedom to create their dream garden.

accomplished by parterres, paths and level changes that are apparent when the garden is seen from above.

My husband and I felt we could include all of these elements in our garden, given the space we had to work with and our temperate microclimate. The back yard faces east and is protected from the prevailing westerly winds. The grade change from the front to the back of the house is so steep that the house is actually three stories at the back. From the rear of the house you can look down on the yard from above. The garden's geometric shapes can be appreciated from our deck off the kitchen, as well as from my husband's office on the second floor (photo, p. 28). We thought that our confined 32-foot by 116-foot rectangular city lot was well suited to the defined edges typical of formal gardens.

We live in the Mission District, the sunniest, warmest part of San Francisco. We get very little fog and are protected from the cold by the Pacific Ocean and the coastal range. Palm trees, lemon trees, geraniums, roses, fruit trees and conifers grow side by side in the Mission District, giving it a distinctly Mediterranean feel. These

After: An angular curb provides the visitor with a physical and mental transition into the secluded courtyard. *(Photo taken at **B** on site plan.)*

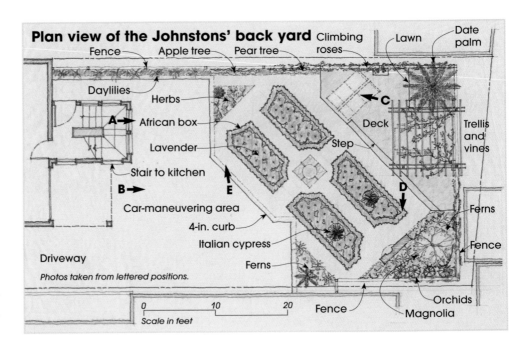

Plan view of the Johnstons' back yard

Fence — Apple tree — Pear tree — Climbing roses — Lawn — Date palm

Daylilies — Herbs

A → African box

Lavender

B → Stair to kitchen

Car-maneuvering area

4-in. curb

Italian cypress

Ferns

Driveway

Photos taken from lettered positions.

← C

Deck — Step

Trellis and vines

D ↓

E ↑

Ferns

Fence

Orchids

Fence — Magnolia

0   10   20

Scale in feet

Photos, from top: Steve Johnston, Delilah Smittle; Illustration: Steve Johnston similarities in climate and vegetation made us confident we could succeed in growing plants common to the Italian Riviera.

Designing the garden

We thought about how we wanted to use the garden and decided we needed a deck large enough for two chaise longues; a table and four chairs; a fountain to muffle city noises; and paths where friends could stroll. We also needed to enclose the yard with a new fence because we planned to demolish the garage and preexisting fence on our property line.

After making a scaled drawing of the lot, we found that we had about 1,000 square feet left for our garden.

We then looked in books and magazines for design inspiration. The most helpful resource was Roy Strong's *Creating Formal Gardens* (Little, Brown, 1989). Steve and I each made sketches of various garden plans. We critiqued each other's schemes and settled on a favorite: a palm tree in the sunniest corner; a pair of espaliered fruit trees and climbing roses along the new fence; an elevated deck with one long step to sit on; an open area for sunning; a trellised area for dining; and a geometric arrangement of parterres. The parterres would be separated by paths intersecting in a circle with a fountain at the center.

On Mother's Day, we invited two friends to brunch and asked them to help us refine our design. April Phillips, a design associate at a local landscape architecture and planning firm and Kimberlee Stryker, a landscape architect, both found the plan strong but too rigid and serious.

By the end of the afternoon, Kim and April had nearly a dozen sketches for us to consider. The design we ultimately chose was the closest to our original scheme but with some terrific improvements. April turned our parterres and paths on the diagonal and made one pair of parterres larger than the other. She also indicated placement of a tree in each of the large parterres. Kim added the missing element to our garden, the *bosco*, by introducing a fern grotto in the corner. Suddenly everything worked. We were now ready to build.

Espaliered fruit trees embrace the courtyard fence, providing all-year interest and a bounty of apples and pears in late summer and fall. *(Photo taken at C.)*

Balancing formality with wildness, the *bosco,* or untamed area, is filled with ferns, cymbidium orchids and a saucer magnolia. *(Photo taken at D.)*

We hired a contractor to cut out part of the concrete driveway and demolish our garage. Then we hired two men with chain saws to cut down the overgrown fence. Those were the only times that contractors worked on the garden. We did everything else.

We began by enclosing the garden with a new fence. All of the wood used in the garden is redwood; it isn't an Italian building material, but it is the best exterior-grade lumber available in California. We ordered the biggest date palm we could maneuver down the driveway from our next-door neighbor, Mark Green, a palm broker. Mark found us a *Phoenix dactylifera* with an 8-foot-tall trunk and a 10-foot-wide crown.

About the same time the palm was delivered, we returned from another trip to Italy with renewed enthusiasm and a plan to put lavender inside all four parterres and a pair of Italian cypress trees in the large parterres. We also decided to build two small boxes into the deck to plant with grapes.

Filling in with plants

After constructing the framework of the garden, we were ready to buy the rest of our plants. We bought an espaliered Liberty apple and an espaliered Seckel pear, and planted them against the south-facing fence (top photo, p. 31).

We purchased a matched pair of 16-foot-tall Italian cypress trees (*Cupressus sempervirens*), which we planted in the large pair of parterres. We put dark green African box (*Myrsine africana*) around the edges of the parterres with deep violet Spanish lavender (*Lavandula stoechas*) in the centers. These plants require similar soil, water and sun conditions, and they are doing well together. In addition, like the palm, they are evergreen in our temperate region, where it rarely goes above 80°F or below 40°F, and will provide interest and texture in our garden all year round.

Celebrating the seasons

We chose cherry-red climbing Dortmund roses for the fence because they are disease-resistant, profuse bloomers that don't mind fog now and then. To make up for their lack of perfume, their deciduous leaves turn a lovely bronze in fall, and their spent flowers develop gorgeous persimmon hips. Contrary to popular belief, we do have seasons here. Many of our plants were chosen to emphasize those changes.

We planted 'Black Monukka' grapes in the small boxes built into the deck. Eventually, they should produce medium-sized, reddish black table grapes. Right now, however, we're more interested in the shade their leaves will provide. In the winter, when we need the heat, their bare vines will let the sun warm the deck.

Because my husband loves them, we planted hybrid daylilies (*Hemerocallis*) next to the apple tree, alternating purple 'Pandora's Box' with red 'Little Maggie'. In the triangular bed at the end of the parterres, we grew kitchen herbs. They have done a little too well, however, and we plan to replace them with roses, a traditional plant for the center of parterres.

We planted a pair of improved Meyer lemons (*Citrus meyeri*) and a Moro blood orange (*Citrus sinensis*) in three large terra-cotta pots, and strawberries beneath the espaliered fruit trees. The honeysuckle vine we cut down with the old fence has already come back. Why fight such a survivor? We're training it along the lattice on our new fence where it attracts hummingbirds.

In the *bosco* we planted Tasmanian tree ferns (*Dicksonia antarctica*), sword ferns (*Nephrolepis*), a saucer magnolia (*Magnolia × soulangiana*)— an impulse buy when it was beautifully in bloom—and sweet violets (*Viola*) as a ground cover underneath a stone bench (bottom photo, p. 31).

Here, in the shadiest part of the yard, we put pale yellow cymbidium orchids that we've had for eight years. They seem to enjoy the company.

Lemon-scented days in the sun

We finished the garden on the vernal equinox and launched it with a garden party, complete with a jazz guitar and alto-sax duo on the deck—which also makes a pretty good stage, as it turns out. Just as we'd envisioned, people sat on the long step of the deck or on the stone bench among the ferns and orchids. The day was warm and full of sun, and the garden made a wonderful place for entertaining.

Now that our work is done, we fight the good fight against aphids, powdery mildew, bitter rot and neighborhood cats. But mostly we just lounge on our chaises and watch the sun glow on the lemons, reminding us of Italy but making us very happy to be right where we are. □

Lemons and oranges bring back Mediterranean memories for the author, who planted these trees in terra-cotta pots to connect the walkways to the espaliered fruit trees at the back of the garden. (*Photo taken at E.*)

Marilyn K. Johnston is a lawyer; her husband, Steve, is an architect.

Even a small space can become a home to a lush, varied garden, and it can provide a relaxing refuge, as well. Author Beaubaire surrounded the patio behind her rented townhouse with colorful annual flowers and a few vegetables. Containers of culinary herbs and annuals give privacy.

A Small Townhouse Garden

Making the most of limited space means breaking the rules

by Nancy Beaubaire

Planning a small garden can be a big challenge. A compact space never seems large enough for the vast horticultural desires of most gardeners. But when you're working in close quarters, you always have to control the inevitable urge to plant more. And you soon discover that the tried-and-true principles of garden de-

sign often don't apply to a modest area.

For anyone who relocates frequently or rents a house or apartment, the challenges of small-space gardening are even greater. We nomadic gardeners dream of beautiful gardens, just as more-settled gardeners do, but often we don't want to invest too much time and money in a garden we might leave soon.

Planning the garden

When I rented a townhouse three years ago, I faced both dilemmas—a small space and a temporary situation. As a

diehard gardener, I was convinced that it was the worst of all possible worlds. Residents of the development where I live are permitted to add personal touches such as gardens or barbecues only behind their townhouse, and must confine these alterations to a 6-ft.-wide by 12-ft.-long concrete patio and the bordering narrow grassy strips. Any changes must be temporary—no concrete footings or mortared pavers, for example.

I longed to plant flowers for cutting, and a few vegetables and herbs. Certainly they would greatly improve the view from my kitchen window and patio, which overlooked a struggling lawn and a weedy wasteland filled with construction debris. As a gardener who was accustomed to much more elbow room, I couldn't imagine cramming everything I wanted to grow in such a tiny area. The first year, I tried to overcome my lack of space by planting a large garden in some friends' yard, a 20-minute commute from my place. I enjoyed the garden, but missed the satisfaction and convenience of having a garden at home. The second year, my landlord agreed to let me plant a small garden in the lawn area beyond my patio, with the stipulation that the garden could be easily removed and the lawn replanted. Planting the area beyond the patio would technically violate the townhouse association rules, but I hoped the garden would look so attractive that everyone would welcome it.

Once I had the go-ahead, I made my plans. I decided to build a raised bed of landscape timbers and enclose it with a low fence made of wooden lattice panels. The raised bed would allow me to bring up the grade of the garden close to that of the patio. Both the timber edging and the fence would establish a visual and physical boundary between the garden and the steep hill beyond. The fence also would give me a feeling of privacy, and, I hoped, keep out critters.

The bed is 14 ft. long, bounded at each end by the existing tall lattice fences that divide my patio from my neighbors'. The garden extends out 3½ ft., leaving just enough flat ground beyond it for anyone who might walk by. With the exception of my neighbors, who regularly come by to admire the garden, this "common area" is virtually unused. I also planted in the narrow areas alongside the tall fences. All told, I have about 55 sq. ft. of in-ground planting space, plus a patio packed with container-grown plants.

Design decisions—In deciding to fill most of the garden with flowers, I realized that annuals were the ideal choice. I could easily and inexpensively grow them from seed. Unlike seed-started perennials, the annuals would bloom the first year. With careful planning, I could count on them to fill in quickly and collectively, and to bloom all season. Growing annuals also meant that I could redesign the garden each year, with no more expense than that of a few seed packets.

Designing the garden perplexed me at first. All the principles that had guided me in designing flower borders in the past didn't quite seem to apply. How could I repeat groupings of the same kind of plant throughout the garden when, compared to any average-size

border, my garden was barely large enough for one grouping? In such a narrow garden, how could I position short and tall plants so they didn't shade each other but didn't line up like soldiers? How could I squeeze in enough flowers so I would have plenty for bouquets and a garden full of flowers, too?

In the end, I abandoned most of the familiar rules and pictured the garden itself as a bouquet, planted with small clusters of different plants. I hoped that this living, ever-changing arrangement also would provide me with a few cut flowers.

To choose flowers, I first indulged myself by writing down all the annuals I wanted to grow, given world enough and time. At this stage, my only restriction was to select those that would be suitable for cutting and would thrive in my site—a windy, southern exposure that's shaded by buildings in the morning and baked in the afternoon. Then I came up with a more realistic list of old reliables that had

Twenty-five wheelbarrowfuls of rotted manure, transported from the front parking lot through the townhouse to the new bed, got the garden off to a good start.

served me well in past gardens: stock, phlox, Shirley poppies, love-in-a-mist, marigolds, zinnias, nasturtiums, cosmos, bachelor's-buttons, flowering tobacco, German chamomile and mignonette. Nearly all of these are excellent cut flowers, have a long bloom period and overlapping flowering times, and would fill the garden quickly with a rainbow of colors. About the only concessions I made to conventional design were to plant more than one of each kind of plant and to place most of the taller plants at the rear of the garden. I still couldn't resist planting a few of my favorite perennials—yarrow, salvia, coreopsis and penstemon—but I managed to hold myself to one plant of each.

I tucked in vegetables and herbs here and there. Tomatoes and cucumbers, trained up poles, and dill marked the ends of the garden. The gray-green broccoli leaves provided a lovely foil to the deeper green cosmos and zinnia foliage. Along the tall fences, I trained sugar snap

peas, bordered by mints, sage, lavender, thyme and bachelor's-buttons; and sweet peas, with stock, phlox and chives beneath. Training plants vertically added growing area and lent a sense of enclosure. Most of my herbs found a home in patio containers: basil, parsley, cilantro, rosemary, lavender, marjoram, oregano and lemon verbena. I also grew pots of vegetables and alpine strawberries.

Building the garden

The logistics of getting some of the materials to the garden called for a creative approach. There is no paved-road access to the rear of the townhouse or to the hilltop where my garden sits. Dragging a mini-tiller, bags of leaves, landscape timbers and fencing up the hill wasn't so daunting, but figuring out how to haul manure up the slope was a little trickier. (I planned to fill the bed with well-rotted manure, which a local farmer gladly let me shovel in my truck for a small fee.) I usually welcome any opportunity to do physical work, but I balked at the thought of pushing the manure uphill, one wheelbarrowful at a time. It just wasn't efficient. That left me with only one alternative: parking my truck out front and maneuvering the wheelbarrow through my living space and out into the garden.

And that's exactly what I did. In several hours' time, I moved a total of 25 wheelbarrowfuls of manure from the truck, up a 1x10 ramp, through the front door, into the living room and the kitchen, out the patio door, down another ramp, across the patio, and into the garden. I felt like the sorcerer's apprentice.

The whole process was not without its taxing moments. To protect the carpeting and tile, I had laid a wide swath of plastic along the entire indoor route. But the plastic frequently slipped out from under the wheelbarrow's tire, threatening the pale-colored carpeting with manure stains. Constantly repositioning the plastic was a nuisance, but necessary. Getting the wheelbarrow onto the ramp leading to the patio was tough, too. The layout of the kitchen prevented me from getting a running start and bouncing the front tire onto the ramp. Instead, I was forced to set the wheelbarrow down each time I reached the ramp and lift the tire onto it.

Even though many of my neighbors were outdoors when I was shoveling the manure, they were surprisingly silent, though I'm sure I was the first and will be the last person to bring anything so earthy into one of these townhouses. When one person did comment that it looked as if I was sprucing things up a bit, I was tempted to tell him that I was planting roses in the living room.

Photo: Roseanne Sabol

Vegetables and herbs find a place amongst the flowers. Here, surrounded by zinnias, the blue-green leaves of kale and a container of basil, the author harvests the white flowers of chamomile for tea.

By the end of the day, the bed looked like a giant dogpen, rather than an attractive site for a garden. I wondered for an instant if gardening here was a mistake, but I didn't really want to turn back. In a corner of my living room, seedlings crowded my propagation shelves, and on the patio, plants filled my knockdown cold frame, all waiting to be planted. So I proceeded to plant, eagerly awaiting the time when I could sit back and enjoy.

Maintaining the garden

Caring for the garden was easy, once I had figured out how to irrigate it. There was no hose hookup within reach, and it was almost impossible to install a spigot outside my townhouse. A watering can worked fine for new transplants, but nothing short of a bucket brigade would have provided enough water for the mature plants, especially those in containers. A garden hose attached to the kitchen-sink faucet with a screw-on portable hose adapter, the kind used to hook up a portable-dishwasher hose, was a simple solution. When I wanted to water the garden, I attached the hose to the faucet and ran it across the kitchen floor and out the pa-

White-flowered tobacco, whose scented blooms open at night, is a favorite annual of the author's.

tio door. Weeding, fertilizing and controlling insects required very little time.

The fruits of my labor

Spring comes maddeningly slow here in Connecticut, compared to California, where I gardened before. So I spaced all my plants much closer than recommended, skeptical that any would reach full size before frost. My concern was un-

founded. The garden began rewarding me with flowers in mid-June, and by mid-July it was bursting with color. Many of the plants, especially the zinnias and flowering tobacco, grew much larger than any I'd ever seen. The small stepping-stones I'd placed here and there were enveloped by lush growth. By mid-season, I could barely squeeze myself onto a small patch of Roman chamomile I had planted as a fragrant seat amongst the flowers.

In the future, I want to plant earlier and include flowers that bloom earlier in the season. I'd also like to try some unusual annuals to complement the more familiar ones. I'll try to leave more room between plants in the garden bed and plant less on the patio—I barely had room for two chairs and a small table among all the containers.

The pleasure my neighbors and I received from the garden made my efforts worthwhile. When I caught a sweet whiff of the flowering tobacco, or harvested fresh herbs for dinner or cut a few flowers for bouquets, it really didn't matter that the garden was temporary and small. ☐

Nancy Beaubaire is an associate editor at Fine Gardening.

Landscaping a Small City Backyard

A retreat far from the madding crowd

by Christopher Cohan

Living amid the asphalt, glass skyscrapers, limited open space and eight million people of New York City, I dreamed for years of having my own garden, a refuge from the noise, smells and constant activity of urban life. As a landscape architect, I was well aware of the challenges of city gardening. Backyards are small and often feel too public. For privacy they usually must be enclosed, but without encroaching on the limited space within. The garden design ought to be intimate and welcoming at the same time. Plants need to be carefully chosen and arranged to create the illusion of more space. And the garden should be designed for low maintenance—even enthusiastic gardeners like me never seem to have enough time.

Fortunately, you can fill a small garden with far fewer plants than a big garden needs, and see almost immediate results. Every detail of a city garden seems to offer special delight, perhaps because of the pleasing contrast with the hardness of the city all around it.

Four years ago, after a long and peaceful walk through Central Park, I returned to my small studio apartment in mid-town Manhattan, my lungs full of fresh air and my mind filled with images of natural splendor. I opened my window, only to be confronted by the boom of a commercial air conditioner, the smell of garlic from a restaurant below and an unobstructed view of solid brick buildings. I knew right then that I needed more green in my life.

My wife, Rita, and I embarked on a real estate search, finally settling on a low-rise brownstone garden apartment in the historic landmark district of Park Slope, Brooklyn. While the real estate salesperson apologized for the weedy, untended backyard and

An informal garden transforms the author's modest city backyard into a peaceful sanctuary. The garden, viewed from the roof, is composed of a diversity of colors, textures and shapes. Nearby trees, such as the trees-of-heaven (right), shelter and partially shade the garden.

Photos, except where noted: Susan Kahn

A multitude of bulbs, including many 'Angelique' tulips, brightens the garden in the early spring.

The central patio is an inviting place for relaxing alone or for entertaining. Viewed from the edge of the patio nearest the living room door, a crabapple, tall shrubs and a barely-visible wood fence frame the garden, creating a backdrop for the woodland-like plantings beneath.

emphasized the amenities of the apartment, I gazed longingly into the sunny, airy yard and began mentally designing a garden. The way I saw it, I was about to purchase a garden that just happened to have an apartment attached to it.

I wanted my garden to be an outdoor room. During nice weather, we would open the large glass doors that lead to the backyard and make the garden an extension of the living room. I hoped to create a retreat where I could quietly relax by myself or occasionally entertain friends. In inclement weather, we would enjoy seeing the garden through windows — a major consideration was the view from the couch in winter.

Evaluating the site

My garden, 25 ft. wide by 40 ft. long, is surrounded by mature plantings of trees and shrubs in the nearby yards. Along with a wood fence at the rear of the property, they provide a backdrop for the garden, creating the illusion that the garden encompasses a much larger space. The trees and shrubs also screen out most of the neighboring buildings, lending a sense of privacy to the space. Behind my yard is a white-flowering crabapple tree, 20 ft. high with an equal spread. Hanging gracefully over the wood fence, it is a glorious shower of white in the spring, and later drops its white, snowflake-like petals on the garden. On the eastern side of the garden are two large, sweet-smelling, rambling roses that clamber over a chain link fence, creating a partial screen. Their repeated explosions of hundreds of small, pink flowers, along with fresh, green foliage, delight the eye throughout the growing season. Several mature yews along the other side of the yard provide year-round greenery and a free-form enclosure.

The garden, which faces south, is sunny from late morning until mid-afternoon, when a nearby silver maple and several Lombardy poplars and trees-of-heaven (Ailanthus altissima) cast a cool, dappled shade. Even more sun falls on the garden once the trees lose their leaves in fall.

Designing and planting

Before I could design the garden, I had to clear debris. This was no small task, since I had to carry everything out of the garden through the apartment. I hauled away a mountain of unwanted stuff—everything from bricks and broken bottles to bicycle tires and waist-high weeds. Just beneath the soil surface, I struck piles of discarded electrical conduit and several pieces of cement, which required three weeks of sledge-hammering to break into easily-removable pieces. I also found a treasure—several slabs of bluestone—enough to pave a small patio and a garden path.

Finally, a little more tired but no less excited, I was ready to make the garden. I chose a simple layout of beds surrounding a centrally-located patio. Between the bluestone slabs, I planted moss, crocus and grape hyacinth bulbs. Compared to a lawn, a paved patio is a much sturdier surface for entertaining and is practically maintenance-free. The patio invites visitors to enter the garden, provides easy access to the beds, gives the garden a focus and affords a close-up view of the plantings.

To keep a clear view year-round from the living room, I set low-growing plants near the doors and taller plants toward the rear of the garden. My main goal in choosing plants was to include a variety of colors, textures, shapes, fragrances and heights, though I avoided any that would look too tall or too large in a small garden. I especially like blue and white flowers and gray-leaved plants, but I didn't limit myself to them. Despite the wide range of plants, I was able to treat them all alike, amending the soil with peat moss, topsoil I saved from digging out the patio, and a balanced fertilizer.

Fragrant plants offer a pleasant welcome to the garden. A bluestone path from the door to the patio is lined with 'Hidcote' lavender, a cultivar with wonderfully fragrant deep-blue flowers. Beneath it grows lemon thyme (*Thymus citriodorus*), which creeps over the edge of the bluestone at the patio entrance and emits a sweet, lemony fragrance when it is crushed underfoot.

A mounded bed, built up from the soil remaining from the patio construction, adds height to the otherwise flat site. Located near the house and in full sun, it's a convenient place for growing culinary herbs. Woolly lamb's-ears (*Stachys byzantina*), snow-in-summer (*Cerastium tomentosum*), sweet alyssum and a border of tasty alpine strawberries hug the ground around the herbs, punctuated by the small, dainty, yellow flowers of Dahlberg daisies (*Dyssodia tenniloba*).

The partially-shaded area at the rear of the garden has a cool and woodsy feeling, which is enhanced by a selection of plants that look as though they belong in a forest understory. Here I painted the fence dark brown so it would fade into the background. A clump of white birch makes a striking contrast against the fence, especially during the winter. In front of them, rhododendron 'P.J.M.' and 'Maximum' and Kurume azaleas make a year-round green foundation and bloom purple, white, and red, respectively, in the spring. Beneath, ferns and pachysan-

Yellow evening primroses and daylilies and pink astilbes (above) draw the eye into the neighbor's patch of daylilies. Astilbes and blue forget-me-nots (below) brighten up a mass of rhododendrons and azaleas.

dra grow among scented, pink-flowering wild geraniums and foxgloves. A butterfly bush (*Buddleia* sp.) in the corner lives up to the promise of its name when its long, purple flowers bring butterflies to the garden in late summer and fall.

A collection of bright flowers fills a sunny bed in front of the rambling roses. In early spring, rosy-pink coral-bells (*Heuchera sanguinea*), white and pink columbines (*Aquilegia* sp.) and yellow St.-John's-wort (*Hypericum* sp.) bloom, followed by yellow daylilies, deep-pink astilbes (*Astilbe arendsii* 'Federsee') and other perennials. This patch of color draws the eye through the garden and beyond the chain link fence into a mass of orange-yellow daylilies that I planted in my neighbor's garden. In midsummer, tall pink and white cleomes open, adding color until late September. These old-fashioned, hardy annuals need little care and reseed readily. The front of the bed is filled with the feathery leaves and gentle pink flowers of cosmos from late July until frost.

In front of the yews, a closely-planted line of rose-of-Sharon keeps the eye in the garden and leads it toward the patio. I've pruned these shrubs into a tight, vertical wall, creating another layer of privacy without taking up too much room. In late summer, their pink flowers enliven the surrounding plantings of rhododendron, azalea, lavender, snow-in-summer and caryopteris.

Large quantities of 'Angelique' tulips, daffodils, jonquils, grape hyacinths, anemones and crocuses announce the beginning of spring throughout the garden. Their flowers are a pleasant distraction from the few bare spots in the garden in early spring. Later on, the cream-edged, ribbed leaves of the many hostas planted here and there contrast dramatically with the deeper green foliage of the surrounding plants.

The garden requires very little work. In the spring, I weed it once, mulch, prune some of the shrubs and fertilize. By summer, all I do is water occasionally, prune plants that have flowered, and enjoy.

Long after the last bloom of the rose-of-sharon has fallen, and the butterflies no longer dance upon the buddleia flowers, I still view my garden with pleasure from the comfort of the couch. Waiting out the long winter, yearning for the first sign of spring, I look out on the garden and smile with pride.□

Christopher Cohan is a registered landscape architect now living in Rye, NY.

A Walled Garden

Outdoor rooms open to the sky

by Angela Overy

Several years ago my husband and I had the opportunity to design a house and garden together as a unit. Our goal was to build a small, intimate garden where we could sit and relax, marvel at sunsets and admire the view, and find haven from the world. We wanted it to wrap around the house and to function as extra rooms where we could live outdoors as much as possible. I dreamed of this small garden as an extension of the living and dining rooms, with similar colors and ambience, so that a vase of flowers on a table inside was just a few feet from the growing flowers outside.

Our site was 25 miles south of Denver, perched on a hill with a magnificent view of the Rocky Mountains. For about 100 years this land had been cattle-ranched by the same pioneer family who are now our neighbors, so the native grasses were cropped but relatively undamaged. Before that, nomadic Arapaho Indians roamed the area, but the land has been fairly untouched by human hands. Scrub-oak-covered hills shelter deer, meadows produce masses of wild flowers, hawks circle overhead, and bluebirds and hummingbirds nest all around. We decided to put the house at the spot of the best view, to build a very small enclosed garden, to develop a transitional area of native plants outside the garden, and to leave the rest totally wild.

Dealing with climate and soil

There were several factors to consider in planning the garden, starting with the climate. Here at 6,000 ft. and just east of the mountains, the weather is mostly hot and dry in summer and cold and dry in winter, occasionally as cold as -30° F. Average annual precipitation is only 14 in., and more than half of that may come as snow.

There are dramatic differences between day and night temperatures; the temperature may change by 30° F in a few hours. On bright, winter days, the earth and

A 4-ft. wall shelters and secludes the author's garden. Plumes of blue fescue and a fiery red heuchera catch the breeze.

outside walls warm up quickly, only to refreeze rapidly at night. Colorado weather is very unpredictable. During the 25 years we've lived here, we've experienced snow in June and roses at Christmas. Many plants can't deal with such conditions.

The winds can roar down the Rockies from the Arctic north, or blow hot and dry, desiccating plants and people. At this altitude, the light is also harsh—24% more ultraviolet rays reach the earth here than at sea level. The growing season is relatively short. Plants usually don't green up until late April, and may die back as early as late September.

Another problem we had to cope with was the soil. Test plugs showed disheartening layers of silty, coarse sand and heavy clay; there was good drainage on some gravelly areas, but painfully hard digging in the patches of clay. This region has never been covered with forest or prairie vegetation, so there's little organic matter in the soil.

Designing the walled garden

My friend and colleague Rob Proctor, a

distinguished artist and plantsman, designed the garden for us. He sketched the initial plan in the time-honored way—on the back of a paper napkin over lunch. The design features two patio gardens, on the north and south sides of the house, connected by a western walkway. We had the contractor build a 4-ft.-high cream-colored stucco wall, which shelters the garden and blends with the stucco house. The architecture has a Mediterranean look, a reminder that our latitude (40° N) is the same as Rome, Madrid and Istanbul. The garden plan provides little shade, so it doesn't interfere with the solar heating of the house. To preserve the view, we'll plant trees only to the northeast and east.

People of many cultures have built walls around their homes to satisfy the human need to define space and to feel secure. On our site, the wall helps to mitigate the vastness of the landscape, and to psychologically anchor the house to the top of the hill. The wall is high enough to protect the plants and to shelter us from the wind, but low enough to preserve the views. We can look up and enjoy the natural light, which is a great feature of Colorado. There is so much sky, and it looks different every hour. At dawn it's soft pink; by noon it's bleached out and dazzling.

The wall echoes the shape of the house, creating the outdoor rooms I wanted and a backdrop for small, interestingly shaped flower beds. The wall holds the heat and creates north- and south-facing areas with different microclimates. Inside the wall, I have a manageable area for altering the soil and humidity, cultivating intensely, and enjoying favored plants in close quarters.

We call the south patio the "winter patio," and bask there in chaises on sunny days in January. Here the summer flowers are cool, restful, pastel colors—soft blues, pinks and yellows. We're attempting to coax grapevines up the slats of an arbor that's shaped like the arched windows of the house. The arbor has a redwood seat, which we cover with plush cushions. In sybaritic moods, I envision lying in the shade picking and munching grapes like

A splashing fountain and pots of petunias and geraniums create a Mediterranean look (above). An arbor with grapevines shades a patio bench (below), where the sitter can admire the fountain and the view beyond. This sun-warmed patio is cozy even in winter.

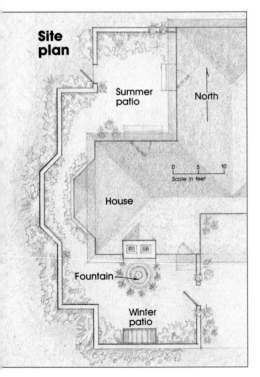

Site plan

Summer patio

North

House

Scale in feet
0   5   10

Fountain

Winter patio

when it rained, lots of mud. Our first job in the garden was to improve the soil. In desperation, we threw the rocks and hunks of concrete under the surrounding scrub oaks. We carted away loads of builder's debris, raked the rough ground to a semblance of order, and then dug a 1-in. layer of Dakota reed-sedge peat into the patio beds. This peat of decomposed reed, sedges and marsh grasses has a high nutrient capacity and a pH of about 7.0 (the same as our soil). It retains moisture well, reducing the need for watering by up to 60%.

We selected plants that need little water and not much attention, that flower readily, and that can withstand climatic extremes. Many of the more successful plants in this area, both native and introduced, are small and compact, with narrow gray leaves. Often their foliage is hairy or waxy, which helps to reduce water loss. We combined some native wildflowers with favorite garden varieties.

In the south patio we planted hardy perennials that make mounds of pastel colors—sprays of pale-violet sea lavender (*Limonium latifolium*), lemon-yellow yarrow (*Achillea filipendulina*) and other mixed pale yarrows (*Achillea millefolium*). The yellow flowers of lavender cotton (*Santolina chamaecyparissus*), complement hazy-blue pincushion flower (*Scabiosa caucasica*). *Coreopsis verticillata* 'Moonbeam' opens pale-yellow flowers most of the summer. More cool-blue perennials that survive here are blue mist spirea (*Caryopteri × clandonensis*), and *Felicia amelloides*, a blue daisy with a yellow center. At the front of the beds, I grow sun roses (*Helianthemum nummularium*), tough little plants with masses of seemingly fragile blossoms of pink, white, yellow and pale-apricot against dark green foliage.

Once the spring bulbs have bloomed and the perennials have started growing, we poke in annuals. On the south patio my favorites are the pink spider plant (*Cleome hasslerana* 'Rose Queen'), and several kinds of *Petunia grandiflora*— 'Azure Pearls', a glorious bluish purple with a white "pearl" inside; 'Azure Sails'; and 'Yellow Magic', all cultivars that don't look like municipal plantings.

On the edge of the beds and along the walkway on the west side we've used very small plants tough enough to tolerate an occasional trodding, tucking them between the sandstone pavers right into the sand, with a little reed-sedge peat mixed in. I'm enchanted by the little plants that thrive in our tough environment. Hen-and-chickens (*Sempervivum* spp.), pinks such as *Dianthus deltoides* 'Zing Rose' and *D. gratianopolitanus* 'Tiny Rubies', and purple rock cress (*Aubrieta deltoidea*) all do well here. Two Colorado natives, pussy-toes (*Antennaria rosea*),

Bacchus, but that hasn't happened yet. There's also a fountain of somewhat preposterous design, but it goes with the grape theme, and the magic sound of trickling water is soothing and luscious in this arid climate. The splashing water also increases the humidity for nearby plants.

The "summer patio" on the north side is shadier. The flower beds abound with hot reds and purples to make an exciting place to sit on summer evenings. Along the western walkway are plants that look good

from the living-room bay window year-round, such as clumps of blue fescue grass (*Festuca ovina* 'Glauca'). All the patio living areas are floored with red Colorado sandstone random pavers, set in sand.

Planting the garden
The surrounding land looked awful when the builder left. There were clumps of concrete dropped by the transit mixer, like cowpats but not so useful as fertilizer; wire, nails and discarded lumber; and,

Illustration: Vince Babak

Along the west side of the house (photo above), the garden wall parallels the projecting shape of the living room's bay window and defines a curving walkway about 7 ft. wide. Clumps of daylilies, blue fescue grass, and Asiatic lilies bloom against the wall. Yellow petunias and red and pink dianthus blossom next to the house. The patio at the north end of the house (photo below) is cool and shady most of the day. The bright flowers of red and purple petunias, penstemons and ice plant are tempered by the soft grey foliage of artemisias and Russian sage.

which really do look like tiny pink and white kittens' paws, and sulphur flower (*Eriogonum umbellatum* var. *subalpinum*) help give the patios an informal look.

The flower beds don't have defined edges. Instead, small plants in front spread over the patio stones. This makes the garden look older than it is. Woolly thyme (*Thymus pseudolanuginosus*) and woolly veronica (*Veronica pectinata*), two grayish-green ground covers you can actually walk on, create an "instant antique" effect in a new garden. Another species, bird's-eye veronica (*V. filiformis*), is perhaps our prettiest creeping ground cover, with little, shiny, green leaves and bright sky-blue flowers.

On the north patio are bright native penstemons—the scarlet bugler (*Penstemon barbatus*) and the purplish *P. strictus.* The shocking-pink flowers of ice plant (*Delosperma cooperi*) splash across the patio, opening and closing with sun and shade. Annual flowering tobacco (*Nicotiana alata* 'Domino Red') and 'Total Eclipse' petunias supply dazzling reds and purples.

Close to the wall are rugged plants that we hope will provide a permanent backdrop over the years. One is a red rugosa shrub rose (*Rosa rugosa* 'Red Grootendorst'). Russian sage (*Perovskia atriplicifolia*) is one of our most attractive and reliable plants—a tall, gray-leaved perennial with flowers in purple spires that last for weeks.

Gardening in four seasons

Like all gardeners we try to extend the season at each end. The patio walls help, but they also create shadows and collect snow, so we have very little new growth until May. Then everything happens very quickly. Extreme heat in midsummer means we have to water at least once a day. Most of the pink and blue flowers are finished by late August, and we're left with yellow and purple wildflowers and garden flowers. In winter, the garden looks empty except for a few gray twigs. The space is still attractive, but very little shows above ground, and we watch the bright bluejays on the patio instead.

In addition to the planting beds, we have many terra-cotta pots, no two planted exactly the same. We move these pots around during the summer according to moods and needs—up the drive to welcome guests, around the fountain to provide a splash of color, up on the wall when we need more room to entertain friends in

the garden. I group favorite pots around a chair outside the kitchen so I can sit and eat lunch surrounded by flowers.

All the pots come indoors in September. A fat Mexican pot of fiesta-colored moss roses (*Portulaca grandiflora*) brightens the kitchen. Tall, elegant pots have pale-pink geraniums (*Pelargonium*), 'Azure Pearl' petunias, cascading blue lobelia 'Sapphire' and green spikes of dracaena (*Dracaena indivisa*). These pots last all winter with regular fertilizing, pruning and pinching back.

Maintaining the garden

Water shortages are a perpetual problem in this area, so we decided not to put in a sprinkler system. Instead we water by hand, drawing as little as possible from the well, and supplementing that with rainfall and snowmelt collected from the roof and stored in rain barrels and a stock pond. Summer storms can be

Tiny plants fit in the crevices between the sandstone pavers. Woolly thyme (left) spreads flat against the rocks. Pussy-toes (top left), hen-and-chickens (center), and sedum (right) grow just a few inches tall.

gullywashers, and at first the runoff from our roof was eroding the hillsides. We thought that by collecting the runoff and releasing it more slowly, we could save water and money. We designed a system that works, but in hindsight, we should have planned this with the architect when the house was designed, coordinating roof lines, gutters and water storage with a drip-irrigation system.

Except where I plant from seed, all the flower beds are mulched with pine-bark chips. The mulch retains soil moisture, reduces weeding, and protects plant roots from the extremes of winter and summer temperatures. Many of our plants wouldn't survive without mulching.

With a very small garden and a short growing season, there's little room or time for seeding new plants or dividing older ones, but I can't resist doing a little of these traditional spring chores. In the summer I fertilize twice a month with solu-

ble fertilizer, and water regularly. After the first few freezes in the fall, I cut back the perennials, leaving the dead stems around the plants as extra mulch. Our winters are mostly so dry that there's little danger of rot or disease. In the spring I inspect for winterkill and prune the roses.

We use no insecticides or herbicides. Grasshoppers could be a problem, but we've encouraged bluebirds by setting out nesting boxes. Each bluebird can eat hundreds of grasshoppers a day, and so far the birds have kept these insects under control. Mice and voles eat a lot of the new spring growth. When I found freshly harvested woolly-veronica flowers outside a mouse hole, I declared war and set a Havahart trap.

Growing wildflowers outside the wall

Scarlet Indian-paintbrush (*Castilleja confusa*), blue larkspur (*Delphinium nelsonii*) and many kinds of penstemons are just a few of the local, native wildflowers. We also have prickly pear and barrel cacti, which seem to me very romantic and cowboyish. The yuccas have big, waxy, bell-shaped flowers that form pale-beige seedpods with large, black seeds inside. In winter the pods make wonderful silhouettes against the vast blue sky, and I pick them for dried-flower arrangements.

Some of the flowers we cultivate inside the wall also grow wild outside, including blue flax (*Linum perenne* subsp. *lewisii*) and cutleaf daisy (*Erigeron chrysopsidis*). The ones inside are slightly larger (but not noticeably healthier) than those outside. East Coast friends ask, "What are you going to do when the grasses and wildflowers grow waist-high?" Here on the high plains they never grow that tall.

Beyond the wall are "experiments"—informal plantings that we hope will survive and reseed, gradually blending in with the native grasses and wildflowers. Starting wildflowers on the disturbed soil has proven difficult. Very few of the varieties in canned wildflower seed mixes meet our demanding conditions of high altitude, low rainfall and poor soil. It's not enough for flower seeds to be casually scattered about. These plants need careful attention to succeed. □

Angela Overy teaches botanical illustration and flower arranging at the Denver Botanic Gardens in Denver, Colorado.

The wall zigs and zags, providing a back-drop for flowers, but never obscures the grandeur of the surrounding landscape.

Enclosing the Garden

How a landscape designer created privacy and interest on a small lot

Shrubs and trees planted along the property lines give the author's 60-ft. by 100-ft. backyard a feeling of seclusion, in spite of nearby neighbors on three sides. Perennial borders flank the lawn, cypresses screen the back of the lot, distant trees provide borrowed scenery and a flagstone path (far right) leads to a secret sitting area and garden pool. (Photo taken at A on site plan.)

by Suzanne Edney

Two summers ago I returned to my garden after a vacation and got a pleasant surprise. The friend who watered my plants had left me a poem about the quiet moments she enjoyed in the garden before facing the cares of the day. I like to think her inspiration was the feeling of enclosure and privacy that, by design, my small backyard provides.

But it wasn't always this way. I started with an open lot, in full view of neighbors on three sides. I screened the property lines with shrubs and trees, made perennial borders, narrowed the lawn at the back to create depth, and hid a sitting area and garden pool behind a group of favorite trees and shrubs. Now I enjoy a spacious-feeling landscape that also offers seclusion. The same design principles I used here can be adapted in your garden.

Assessing the site

When I moved to Cary, North Carolina, seven years ago, the 60-ft. × 100-ft. backyard both disturbed and encouraged me. I most lamented the lack of privacy. There was a heavily-traveled road on the far side of the right-hand neighbor's bare lot, and a shady, barren backyard on the left. To the rear, I could see two more lots and one-story houses whose roofs I would eventually have to hide by growing tall plants on the back property line.

Apart from being fully exposed, our property had two other inherited drawbacks. There was a home-built, brown storage shed in one back corner of the lot. It would take me five years to realize I could camouflage this regrettably sound and ugly structure with vines. The second eyesore was a chain link fence surrounding the yard. It was handy for containing my fox terrier and excluding neighborhood foot traffic, but it was very unattractive.

Happily, there were some good things about the property. One was deep soil, undisturbed for many years—a blessing here in the Piedmont of North Carolina, where most land has only 2 in. of topsoil. This meant that I could count on quick growth from my plantings. Also, the backyard was large enough for me to create several separate areas of interest, but small enough for me to handle alone (I'm the only gardener in my family). The lot sloped gently away from the house, making it easier for me to design a garden that looked deep. I could add screening plants, with perennial borders in front of them, and still have room for a lawn and other features. And there was already just the right number of specimen trees to anchor the design. In the neighboring yards were other attractive trees that I planned to "borrow" views of. The shaded yard to the left, with a number of dogwoods and redbuds, was dominated by a gorgeous old sweet gum. The lot to the right would give me the pleasure but not the worry of a 15-year-old white pine. (White pines suffer in our hot summers.) There were also a juvenile willow oak and mature pines towering over all three properties, but allowing plenty of sun below.

The neighboring properties were rentals, so I contacted the landlords between yearly occupants and offered to improve their lots in ways that would enhance my own. For example, I used free composted leaves from the city to make a bed alongside the noisy road, and planted a buffer of dogwood seedlings and give-away plants from local organizations.

Designing the garden

Though my first priority was planting strategic areas of the property line for quick screening, I knew that "quick" in reality meant three to five years, so I would also have to consider other desires and work them into the design. I decided to create a feeling of depth by shaping the lawn to narrow gradually as it approached the back of the lot, and by using plants with bold, colorful leaves near the house and small-leaved plants in the distance. I also wanted a surprise at the rear of the garden, and several distinct areas to walk through. I intended to attract birds with the gentle sound of water and with plants for nesting sites and food. The garden had to have fragrance. To direct scents toward seating areas, I planned to take advantage of the wind patterns. Bright pops of color and subtle contrasts of foliage would catch the eye in different parts of the garden throughout the seasons. Because I'm a landscape designer, I would also use my garden to evaluate new plants.

Screening the property

Before I planted anything, I camouflaged the offending chain link fence.

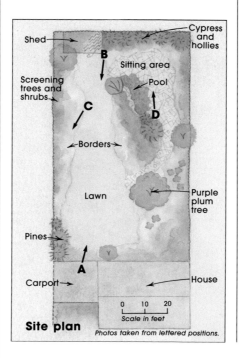

Site plan

Shed
B
Sitting area
Cypress and hollies
Screening trees and shrubs
Pool
C
D
Borders
Lawn
Purple plum tree
Pines
A
Carport
House

0 10 20
Scale in feet

Photos taken from lettered positions.

To make the poles all but disappear, I painted them with Rustoleum brown primer. I could have used a flat black or a hunter green, but with a woodland on the left, I chose brown. I planned to erase the chain links by training ivy through them. But in the meantime I devised an American version of the wattle fences of the United Kingdom by weaving dead branches into the links. The branches made a brush-like background that looked quite natural.

I started the screening and background for the garden by replacing some of the shrubs and trees on the property lines. Along the back, I sawed down a glossy privet (a small-tree-sized relative of common privet) to make room for the taller, evergreen spires of Leyland cypresses and a 'Nellie R. Stevens' holly, which would one day hide the rooftops beyond. Out went a number of diseased camellias in one corner, to be replaced by several plants: 'Nellie R. Stevens'; wintersweet (*Chimonanthus praecox*), which is a Chinese shrub with fragrant flowers that appear before the leaves, often in late winter; and a Japanese viburnum, *V. dilatatum*, with 5-in. flower clusters that appear in spring. I surmised that the young willow oak along the right property line would someday create shade and root competition, so out it came and in went a 'Trident' maple, a less vigorous tree. Usually planted in the Northeast, the 'Trident' maple was purely experimental in this part of the country and, I'm happy to say, doing beautifully after five years.

To get an idea of plants that do well in your area, I recommend you check older neighborhoods. In a

The backyard is enclosed by plants on three sides and screened at the front by the house and a board fence topped by lattices and planters. (Photo taken at B on site plan.)

Illustration: Lainé Roundy

Seasonal color brightens one of the author's perennial borders, while the shrubs in back obscure the chain link fence. In the foreground, the broccoli-like flower clusters of sedum 'Autumn Joy' are weeks away from blooming. (Photo taken at C on site plan.)

20- to 30-year-old neighborhood, I happened on a tall, leggy thing with wonderfully fragrant flowers in February. The plant was in a shaded spot, so I decided its lanky habit was happenstance. I soon learned that I'd found a honeysuckle from China, *Lonicera fragrantissima*. I acquired one and vowed to keep it looking full. The books said it grew to 10 ft. by 10 ft., and after six years of careful pruning, I see their predictions were correct. Each spring, after the new branches have had a chance to grow, I coax this honeysuckle into shape. I say coax because one false move with my clippers, and I have a hole that I will see for the rest of the summer. Guided by the new growth, I maintain my shrub in a lovely, soft, rounded form. I paired the honeysuckle with a shrub I saw at a local public garden, *Illicium parviflorum*. Both plants have similar foliage texture, with medium-sized leaves. They make an interesting combination, with the honeysuckle's branches arching out and down, cascade-fashion, and the star anise branches all pointing skyward.

I planted the honeysuckle and star anise mid-way along the left property line to head a perennial border that runs back to the shed, and to begin the narrowing of the lawn that helps give the yard the illusion of depth that I wanted. Unfortunately, the location does have a drawback. I wanted to enjoy the fragrance of the honeysuckle in late winter, but I forgot that our winds tend to shift as early as February. Instead of wafting through

A bluish *Chamaecyparis pisifera* 'Squarrosa' and Leyland cypresses screen the secret sitting area at the back of the garden. (Photo taken at D on site plan.)

the patio, the honeysuckle's sweet smell blows toward our neighbors in the back.

Next to the honeysuckle and star anise I wanted a uniform planting to set off the 10-ft.- to 12-ft.-deep perennial border. I planted a 10-ft.-long hedge of bridal-wreath (*Spiraea × vanhouttei*), a small, flowering shrub. The plants were cheap—a dozen for $6.99. How could I lose? Well, I'll tell you how. In three years, the plants completely hid the fence, but over the next two years, they deteriorated

badly. I admit I never pruned this hedge, but I am convinced that the placement of these plants was wrong from the beginning. They were starved for light.

Six years after planting, I had to pull out the bridal-wreath hedge and replant. My choice this time was a broad-leafed, evergreen, native shrub, *Leucothoe populifolia*. I'd planted one nearby several years earlier and had seen it grow a spectacular 3 ft. per year. This time I feel quite confident I've made the correct choice of "right plant, right place."

To finish screening the left property line, I planted a mix of small shrubs, most of them 4 ft. to 5 ft. tall, just high enough to mask the fence. Near the patio, I set a cutleaf Japanese maple and a Rocky Mountain juniper (*Juniperus scopulorum*); several deciduous shrubs, including a snowberry (*Symphoricarpos × chenaultii*), a filbert from Japan (*Corylus gotoana*); a graceful, flowering shrub from Japan called *Deutzia scabra*; and several broadleaf evergreens, including a holly grape (*Mahonia bealei*), a member of the tea family called *Ternstroemia gymnothera*, an Alexandrian laurel (*Danae racemosa*), and a Florida anise (*Illicium floridanum*). The combination has proven to be rich in texture and color, a welcoming sight when you enter the garden from the patio. Near the shed at the back of the yard I planted a Japanese rose (*Kerria japonica*) and a strawberry shrub (*Calycanthus floridus*).

Instead of screening the right property line directly, I partitioned the yard with a planting of shrubs and trees that starts near the house and runs back towards the shed, narrowing the lawn on the way. For a low, loose hedge, I planted a shrub euonymous with yellow-variegated leaves, *Euonymous japonica* 'Variegata'. I set taller plants along the hedge, including a Japanese cedar (*Cryptomeria japonica*), a blue false cypress from Japan called *Chamaecyparis pisifera* 'Boulevard', and a purple smoke tree, *Cotinus coggygria* 'Purpureus', which I've pollarded (see the sidebar on the opposite page) to keep small and to show off its beautiful, round leaves. In front of the partition planting is another perennial border.

Partitioning the yard this way also completely screens one of its back corners. From the patio, visitors think they can see the whole garden, but they can't. Out of sight is a secret flagstone sitting area and a small pool. To find the pool, visitors can follow the lawn back to the shed and turn around the smoke tree, or head toward the right property line where a flagstone path curves out of sight under the spreading branches of a large, purple plum tree. Between the plum tree and the fence, a distance of 20 ft., I planted low shrubs and woodland plants. Some earlier owner had planted 'Pink Pearl' azaleas along the fence in marching formation. I love their soft pink blossoms, so I lifted the plants and set them under the plum tree in a more natural pattern. I also planted four varieties of rabbiteye blueberries for the birds (honestly, it never occurs to me to harvest the fruits myself), and a number of shrubs and trees along the right property line to accompany the 'Trident' maple, and to screen the pool and sitting area.

Screening the patio

Originally, the patio was open to the driveway and the street on one side, and a neighboring house on another side. I installed a board-on-board fence, slatted so that air could circulate to the deeply-shaded beds along its base. The fence has two 4-ft. gates which open onto the driveway for bringing in supplies. One year the neighbors cut off the lower limbs of their dogwood trees, which had provided beautiful screening at the top of the fence. So much for borrowed greenery. To restore privacy, I added a planter on top of the fence. In the planter I use drought-tolerant perennials such as 'Autumn Joy' sedum, ribbon grass (*Phalaris*), and a small spurge (*Euphorbia robiae*), as well as a few annuals for flower color through the summer. If cold kills any plants, I can replace them easily with divisions from my garden in spring.

Maintaining seclusion

The privacy I want in my garden obliges me to keep plants growing in crowded conditions. The Leyland cypresses may be too close together already. I've had to treat them for bagworms, and the lower limbs seem to be slowly thinning. Eventually I will have to either remove every other tree, or set low screening plants beneath them. I may try a friend's recommendation, a fern which I'm told will grow 4 ft. tall in heavy shade and spread to colonize an area. I've also heard I can pull it up easily if I don't want it anymore.

I budget pruning time in spring to keep many plants in scale with my small backyard. I cut back some plants by half each year, after they bloom. The 'Trident' maple desperately wants to be a shrubby thing, but I manage to cut sprouts and suckers from its five beautiful trunks each spring to make it look like a tree. The ivy woven into the fence is a rousing success. All I do each year is lift the runners that head into the perennial beds and weave them through the chain links.

I see changes in the garden with every bit of maintenance, and I welcome them. I see my mistakes as adventures and as excuses to grow new and untried plants for the on-going creation that I call my garden. When I have to fill yet another void where one of my beloved experiments has failed, I remind myself that patience is a virtue. All my efforts are more than repaid when I share the serenity and seclusion of the garden with my family and friends. □

Suzanne Edney is a landscape designer in Cary, North Carolina.

POLLARDING MAKES A SHRUB-SIZED TREE

Of all the plants I prune each year to keep my crowded garden in shape, the most striking is a purple smoke tree (*Cotinus coggyrgia* 'Purpureus'). I planted it for its stiff, purple leaves arranged in rows along the branches, but in the second year of its growth I was astonished and dismayed to see that most of the new leaves were out at the tips of the first year's growth. Without pruning, the branches would eventually spread 5 ft. to 10 ft. in all directions, much too wide for the space available. I trimmed the tree back to 4-ft.-tall trunks and was rewarded with at least three fast-growing branches from the top of each trunk, all loaded with beautiful leaves.

A forest of 8-ft. to 10-ft. branches ascends from the low trunks of a pollarded purple smoke tree. The author cuts the branches off at their bases each year to achieve this effect and to keep the tree small.

Since then, I've maintained the 4-ft.-tall trunks and cut the branches back to their bases every winter. Year by year, the trunks thicken, and so do their knobby tips, where the branches arise. Also, more branches sprout each spring. This winter, after six years of pruning, I removed about 50 branches.

The name for this kind of pruning is pollarding. It's often practiced with park and street trees to keep them a suitable size. If you start pollarding when a tree is young, you can maintain its size indefinitely. You should not, however, cut the top off an older tree in an effort to start pollarding—a large topping cut leads to decay.

It's a pleasure to watch the smoke tree change with the seasons. In early spring the knots on the ends of the trunks begin to sprout, and, in a week's time, the small, new shoots, with their unfolding leaves, give the plant the look of a newly-clipped poodle. The branches grow straight up with great speed in spring and are soon 8 ft. to 10 ft. tall. Upright and crowded together, they form a dense and distinctive screen. (My tree helps hide a secret sitting area and a small garden pool). By the end of the summer, the leaves have lost much of their glorious color to the high night temperatures of the South. But as fall temperatures drop, the leaves turn a striking orange. Once the leaves fall, the tree looks almost like a sculpture, with a forest of branches atop thick trunks. —*S.E.*

Landscape as Living Space
Harmony and color for a Southwest garden

When Carol and Frank Naylor aren't working in their garden, they're using it as an
outdoor living and entertaining area.
Here, the rose walk and upper gardens
embrace a small lawn and covered patio, with dramatic views of mountains to
the west. As seen from the crest of the
ridge in the light of a dramatic sunset,
roses, sweet alyssum, and blue and white
salvias glow in the last light of day.

All photos, except where noted: © Terrence Moore

by Carol and Frank Naylor

We love to garden. We consider our garden not just a place to grow plants but also a living area and a place to entertain. Our garden wraps our home with color, inviting us outdoors and blurring the traditional boundaries between house and garden. We also love the desert—not only its plants but its animals, too—and we wanted a garden where all are welcome, wild and tame alike. Combining these passions, we've created a home where our interest in gardening and our respect for the desert work together, without threatening each other. We've created garden areas that expand our living quarters—not just garden rooms but real extensions of our home.

Our house sits on a one-acre lot nestled in the Carefree Foothills north of Phoenix, Arizona, overlooking the Valley of the Sun. Except for a few queen palms, the landscaping was nonexistent when we moved in five years ago—a veritable canvas just waiting for our ideas to give it form and color. The desert had been left undisturbed except where construction crews had taken their toll. We wanted to preserve all of the remaining desert, using only a small portion of the construction-disrupted site for the garden and restoring the remainder to its previous condition.

We envisioned our gardens as an ever-changing environment that would never bore, and one that would provide us with a limitless supply of weekend projects to work on. But what we didn't want was something so overwhelming that it would keep us from enjoying restful times.

Here in USDA Zone 9, winter lows drop to the teens and summer highs reach the upper 90s and low 100s. Thanks to the surrounding foothills and our 2,650-ft. elevation, we have more rainfall than nearby Phoenix, an average of 16 in. a year. In all the garden areas we installed some form of irrigation. Because of the high calcium content of our water, which clogs drip systems, we use sprinklers and bubblers. In some areas the soil consists of a 2-in. to 3-in. layer of sand and gravel topsoil over a base of partially decomposed granite. Although sandy, the soil is rich in iron and other nutrients. Adding phosphate and mulch provides fertile ground for planting.

We must choose plants carefully that will withstand summer and winter extremes. We've limited the number of trees we've added, confining them to the desert areas of our garden, and selecting native varieties almost exclusively. In addition to this, we have a number of wild creatures to deal with. Rabbits can devour a garden in one night, and pack rats will cart away hundreds of dollars' worth of plants to add to their dens.

Renewing the desert

The majority of our lot lies north and south of the house and east to the street, encompassing about 10,000 sq. ft. of virgin Sonoran Desert. An area in front of the house of roughly 2,000 sq. ft. had been cleared during construction for the installation of utilities and the septic tank. When we first moved in, this entire area was landscaped in what many people consider "desert landscaping": crushed granite spread over denuded and sanitized ground to a thickness of 2 in.

Anyone who has ventured into the natural beauty of the Sonoran Desert knows that this is a far cry from the often lush growth one finds in the Foothills area. The region is heavily contoured with ridges and washes (arroyos); native vegetation includes cacti and shrubs with names like "fairyduster" and "brittlebush." Palo verde and mesquite trees grow 15 ft. to 20 ft. high and about as many feet across. Some desert plants bloom year-round, but spring is the most colorful time, with pinks, purples, yellows, reds, oranges and whites. The palo verde burst into a bright-yellow bloom in June and the desert

Formerly a sea of gravel, the front area is now a colorful garden. In the raised bed, roses, chrysanthemums, yuccas and Texas sage brighten the entryway. Against the house, the climbing rose 'Pinata' blooms year-round. To the right, cacti and native plants reintroduced by the authors have become established. The bench at center is a good vantage point for viewing wildlife feeding under the palo verde tree.

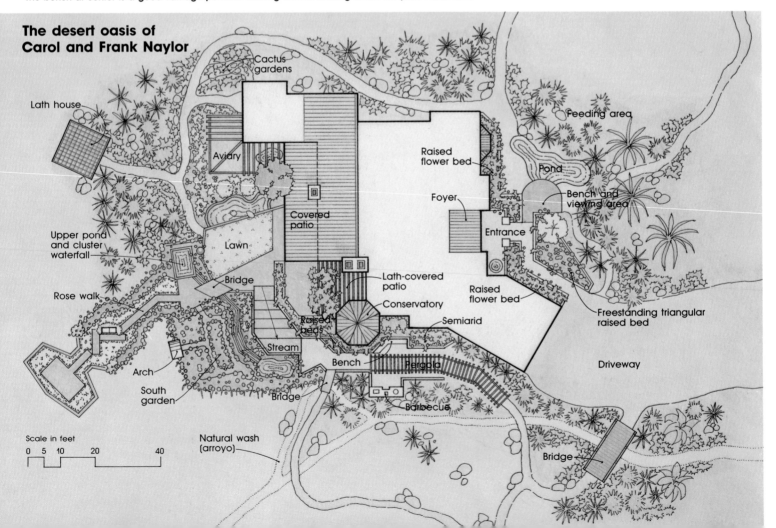

The desert oasis of Carol and Frank Naylor

Cactus gardens

Lath house

Feeding area

Aviary

Raised flower bed

Pond

Foyer

Bench and viewing area

Covered patio

Upper pond and cluster waterfall

Lawn

Entrance

Bridge

Lath-covered patio

Rose walk

Conservatory

Raised flower bed

Raised beds

Semiarid

Freestanding triangular raised bed

Stream

Bench

Arch

Pergola

Driveway

South garden

Bridge

Barbecue

Scale in feet
0 5 10 20 40

Natural wash (arroyo)

Bridge

looks like a carpet of yellow all month.

We planted cuttings of prickly pear, cholla, small saguaros, pincushion, ocotillo and barrel cacti in the graveled area, and placed large rocks throughout. This area is slowly reverting back to its natural state, and forms the transition zone between the gardens near the house and the natural desert.

Adding color

We wanted to accent the front of the house with plants and flowers, and we also wanted to encourage wild creatures to inhabit the area. We built a series of raised flower beds using slump block, which is like a cross between a concrete block and a large adobe brick. The beds extend along the front of the house for 100 ft., are 3 ft. wide and 18 in. deep, and contain topsoil enriched with mulch and ammonium phosphate. A triangular center bed is planted with roses, chrysanthemums, Texas sage and yucca, and is bordered with blue salvia and evergreen hedges. The mums bloom twice a year, providing spectacular color combinations from May through June and again from late October through December. Most of the roses start blooming in early April and continue until late December, when the first daffodils begin pressing up from the earth. By March this bed is a sea of yellow daffodils interspersed with blue German irises and nierembergia.

Along the front walls of the house, rows of Louisiana irises, Shasta daisies, geraniums, begonias, alyssum and tree roses create a more formal appearance. Lantana in purple, white, yellow and orange complements the colorful climbing rose 'Pinata', which blooms majestically 12 months of the year. We like to add a few agapanthus, delphiniums and snapdragons to attract the hummingbirds that are year-round residents, but we need to protect these delectable plants with wire from the foraging rabbits. Other plants scattered in this area include rosemary, lilacs and aloe.

Inviting wildlife

We're avid bird-watchers, and we wanted to make a sanctuary. The easiest way to do this is to provide that rare but essential elixir in the desert: water. We dug a free-form pond, 20 ft. by 6 ft. by 2 ft. deep, the old-fashioned way, with pickax and shovel. After lining the bottom and sides with chicken wire, we plastered it with 3 in. of cement. Once the cement had cured, we coated the inside with Q-Bond, a product that combines plaster with fiberglass and completely seals leaks. The pond follows the top of a hill and curves around a palo verde tree, which provides cover for the animals that use our feeding area.

Animals and birds are attracted to the

Tree roses and Oriental lanterns lend formality to the garden surrounding the aviary. The pond acts as a moat, helping to keep wildlife out of the lawn area. This garden gives almost continuous color throughout the year.

The sound and sight of running water are soothing, particularly in Arizona's dry climate. The pastel colors of irises, showy Mexican primroses, sweet alyssum and salvia crowding around the stream enhance its cooling effect.

pond like mad! Rabbits, squirrels, chipmunks, coyotes and javelinas appear regularly. The occasional mountain lion, bobcat and mule deer pay a casual visit to our feeding grounds. Gambol quail, orioles, cardinals, thrashers, doves, woodpeckers, finches, cactus wrens and blue jays are just a few of the many birds we've identified. Of course, with this variety of small animals around, we also see predators such as horned owls, vultures, hawks and rattlesnakes.

We encourage wildlife by putting out regular feedings of dry dog food, cracked corn and vegetable scraps. A bench between the pond and the triangular garden and about 20 ft. from the feeding area makes an excellent viewing spot, distant enough to provide the animals with the comfort zone they need. Low-voltage lighting allows us to watch as our visitors eat their midnight snacks. The pond has also given us, as an added bonus, room to acquire water plants—irises, cattails, papyrus, water lilies and umbrella plants.

Designing the aviary and surrounding garden

The backyard from the end of the patio was undeveloped, though areas of the natural desert had been damaged during construction. The ground on either side of the patio drops off considerably, leaving a level area of only 15 ft. by 25 ft. The kitchen, conservatory, living room and master bedroom open onto the patio, and we wanted to expand this area without obstructing the spectacular view to the west of Black Mountain, a 3600-ft. remnant of an extinct volcano, and without using brick or other heat-holding materials. We also wanted to incorporate garden areas that would hug the house, softening the look and providing some shade. And we needed an aviary to house our ever-growing collection of birds and pet rabbits.

The aviary was our first priority. The L-shaped structure wraps around the master suite, and is protected from summer heat and winter's dry cold. It is designed more to keep predators out than to keep our birds in. Inside, covered feeding troughs hold a three-day food supply. A waterfall and pond supply fresh, circulating water; a float device senses when the level drops, and the pond is automatically topped up. A brick walk runs the 40-ft. outside circumference and allows visitors a closer look. Each morning we awake to the gentle songs of the finches, and our evenings are softened with the cooing of the turtledoves.

For the gardens surrounding the aviary, we built retaining walls of scrap block, plastered with a mixture of mortar and sand to hide irregularities and painted to match the house. The gardens control the erosion that was occurring on the slope, and they soften the hard lines of the aviary.

We planned for color and fragrance year-round and for cut flowers to use in arrangements. Roses bloom from April through December, and chrysanthemums thrive in the warm days and cool nights of spring and fall; together, these plants weave a tapestry of color along the winding path that leads to the cactus garden. Their sprawling growth habit shades the roots of neighboring plants, and so helps retain moisture in the beds.

Tree roses grace the semiformal appearance of the upper garden, and Shasta daisies, geraniums, daylilies, alyssum, 'Torchglow' bougainvillea, ruellia and lycoris bloom from May through November. In early February, hyacinths, daffodils and freesias begin to open. Oriental lanterns accent this bed.

A covered patio spans the back of the house, just off the living room and master bedroom. Here we wanted a grassy area for our dogs to romp, and we needed to extend the patio seating area for larger gatherings. For visual interest, as well as water sounds, we built a pond and fountain that overflow into a small streambed winding along the south stairs and through the south side garden into another pond. A brick path edges the lawn area and continues over the stream and out onto the crest of the ridge, the highest spot in our garden. Here the path is lined with a large variety of tea and floribunda roses bordered by vinca in summer and daffodils in spring. Various cacti back the roses, and the contrast is striking when both are blooming. The path ends with a seating area and a magnificent view of the mountains to the west, north and east and of Phoenix to the south. This is our favorite spot to watch developing summer thunderstorms.

Planting the hillside

The ground drops away steeply to the south from the lawn and rose path. Summer downpours were wreaking havoc on this hillside—great amounts of topsoil disturbed during construction were being washed away. Brick stairs trimmed with railroad ties descend from the lawn along the south end of the patio. Using in-

teresting rocks we'd collected over the years, we divided the area along the stream into four sections, each separated by a small brick walkway. We added a lattice-work arch on the far western side and planted a row of prickly pear cactus to define the perimeter of the garden from the natural desert.

This garden has an English flavor to it. It's most colorful in spring, when spires of hollyhocks and delphiniums form the background for tulips, irises, daffodils, petunias, pansies and other plants. Rose standards, 'Mr. Lincoln' and 'Love', are focal points of the front sections. Alyssum reseeds exuberantly and forms a year-round ground cover. We're also trying our hand at topiary, and already the definite lines of a rabbit, squirrel, cat and mouse can be seen. Cool colors predominate in summer—white, pink and lavender, provided mostly by alyssum and *Vinca minor*. Fall is spectacular. Roses produce abundantly in the cool nights and warm days, and chrysanthemums line the stairs with a bank of color that illuminates the darkest night. In winter our topiary friends become the prominent features in the landscape. By January, hyacinths, daffodils and crocuses are producing their first flowers of the season.

Building the pergola

By far the most challenging project has been the pergola, which is still under construction. The south side of the house was our biggest eyesore. The windowless 20-ft. by 40-ft. garage wall reflected heat onto the desert floor, literally cooking the tough native flora. Subjected to the reflected heat, the conservatory was unbearably hot in summer. We needed a way to cool down this area without obstructing the view. A pergola, we figured, would shade and solve the overheating problem. With its parallel colonnade, open roof of girders, and canopy of flowers and vines, the pergola would make a covered walk as well, and give interest to an otherwise blank wall. We were intrigued with a pergola we had seen in England at Gravetye Manor, and decided to adapt its design to our gardens.

The site rolled and curved, following the natural lay of the land and the walls of the house. Building a structure that curved sounded more interesting than making a straight, level pathway. The top of the pergola would remain level. The pergola is 8 ft. wide and 40 ft. long. The walkway underneath is 5 ft. wide. We dug footings 1 ft. in diameter and 18 in. deep for the main posts, which are five pairs of 4x6 fir timbers, cut to various heights to conform to the rolling site. We set the posts approximately 10 ft. apart on the concrete footings and held them in place with rebar. Crossbeams extend 18 in. on either side of the pergola, pro-

viding some shade and support for plants. Timbers 10 ft. long run the length of the pergola, connecting the crossbeams. A "roof" is created by 2x4s, placed on edge and spaced 2 in. apart, fanning out around the corners. The pergola is 7 ft. high where it meets the retaining walls, so it doesn't obstruct the view from the conservatory. Instead, the architecture creates visual interest from the conservatory windows above, as well as from the walk below.

Next we tackled the barbecue area. Built of slump block and painted to match the house, it incorporates a gas grill, a smoker and a sink with running water. Under the counter is storage space for charcoal. Wood framework supports the smoker and barbecue. The top is finished in matching ½-in.-thick flagstone. Eventually we plan to expand the pergola to provide partial shade to this area. The pathway in this section is a 2-in. layer of concrete, sprinkled liberally with gravel and lined with red brick.

Planting the walkway

We used blues and pinks to give the pergola a cool feeling. 'Simplicity' hedge roses line the pathway and grow in the beds under the conservatory windows. Their height and free-blooming, self-cleaning habit make them the perfect choice for low-maintenance color. Along the pergola we planted 'Blue Girl' and 'Blaze' climbing roses, wisteria, mandevilla 'Alice du Pont', and bougainvillea 'Barbara Karsh'. The ground there was bedrock; our solution was to excavate a 3-ft. by 2-ft. hole for each plant, and to use a bubbler system for irrigation. We know from experience that the bedrock drains just slowly enough to create a "flowerpot" effect, reducing the amount of water needed. Blue salvia grows in between the climbers. A delightful bonus is wild datura, which sprang up as a volunteer and weaves its way among the plantings. The datura has deep blue-green leaves and huge, white, trumpet-shaped flowers that turn into round, spine-covered seedpods.

The retaining beds surrounding the conservatory are high enough to discourage rabbits, so we grow plants here that we can't elsewhere—petunias, lobelia, irises, stock, sweet peas, phlox and, in summer, geraniums and dahlias. Bougainvillea, rosemary, Texas sage and night-blooming cereus also grow here.

We're amazed at the results of this project. This area is an oasis, comfortable even on the most stifling days, where petunias bloom happily into August. The shade thrown by the pergola cools the air a good 10°F. In winter the site is sheltered from cold winds. □

Carol and Frank Naylor garden near Phoenix, Arizona.

Annuals, perennials and roses grow in profusion along the streambed and stairs in the south garden. English-style plantings, southwestern architecture and Mexican terra-cotta ornaments result in an unlikely mix that's unique and exotic.

Even in December, gardens wrap the authors' home with color, invite the viewer outdoors, and soften the traditional boundaries between indoors and out. Bougainvillea drapes the covered back patio, spilling into the lavender lantana and chrysanthemums growing along the streambed.

To create a transition zone from the gardens to the natural landscape, the authors planted roses at the edge of the hillside garden, backed by prickly pear cacti. In flower, the two make an unusual combination. The gray-green shrub at the upper right is a soap tree (*Yucca elata*).

Viewed through grape leaves, an Australian tree fern leads to the author's sanctuary. At the foot of the fern is curly ivy; to the left is asparagus fern; and to the right, climbing the fence, is gold-dust ivy. (Taken at A on site plan, p. 56.)

Sheltered by a loquat tree, the ivy-covered sanctuary gate anchors one end of a viney wall. To the right of the gate are the rose 'Cécile Brunner', Hall's honeysuckle, Cape honeysuckle, an Australian brush cherry tree and a passionflower. (B)

Ferns and ivy comfort the author in early spring before vines knit a canopy over his head. (C)

A Vine Sanctuary
Gardener finds peace of mind in a leafy bower

by K. Mose Fadeem

The spirit of post-modern civilization prods me periodically into an awful rush of avoidance behavior, and I need a place in which to be quiet and insular. So it is that on this thin sliver of California coast I've developed a small trellised enclave where I take respite as a frequent exile among the vines.

The climate here is everything one would expect of the coast—temperate, unpredictable, foggy. Protection from winds and salt spray is a clear necessity. Unable to afford or scavenge material for stone walls, I found in vines the architectural potential to screen my small house and studio. Following the discovery of such an elastic barrier, the development of the sanctuary was a matter of time, patience, observation, floundering and fate. The best advice I ever received on gardening came from a friend and bamboo enthusiast many years ago: Take your time, don't try to do it all at once.

At the start there was only an old 'Concord' grape on an arbor built of scrap wood, pipes and angle iron; nearby was a loquat tree, and the rest was 7-ft. weeds. Clearing the weeds, I removed the roots and turned the rest into the sandy soil, adding some dried manure. Just at that time a friend was changing residence and asked me to move her entire garden. In return I could keep some of the plants. Silky wisteria, Cape honeysuckle and Australian brush cherry came from that garden. Soon after, a rambling 'Cécile Brunner' rose and a honeysuckle arrived as gifts. The sanctuary and I were on our way to vine heaven (Nirvina?).

As the vines shaped the sanctuary, they slowly shaped my views as well; that is, if one can imagine a mentality as effusive as vines. There was no plan or design. I was compelled to simply gather vegetative material and then feel my way amongst the goo of it all, something like "expressionist gardening." Today, six years later, some two dozen vines make up the walls of the sanctuary and give the garden its character, the precise nature of which still eludes me. I named it "Mulchdown."

One peculiar quality about Mulchdown is that you can't view it all at once. The landscape is never farther than a few feet away, and while pieces of it may be examined, there is no single encompassing viewpoint by which the whole garden might explain itself. What is immediate is the uninhibited vigor of vines colliding, thrusting obliquely with the shuffling manners of barbarians. The result is a living tapestry rich in texture. It's a physically and psychologically enveloping affair—one wears this garden like a tweedy garment.

Because they struggle for light and air and do it all over something else, vines are said to be "aggressive." Vines, though admittedly loquacious, are no more or less aggressive than any other plant that does what it can to survive—a crowded pansy will push and shove as best it can to ensure its purpose. Nonetheless, vines remain in the minds of many a paradigm of the furious will to succeed. They are superb opportunists, taking advantage of other life forms and using them for their own ambitions. They cling, climb and sometimes smother with such healthy energy that one begins to understand this behavior as an expression of the spirit.

Perhaps vining is an opportunity to contact other life forms—vines do a lot of touching. You cannot enter the sanctuary without immediately participating in the

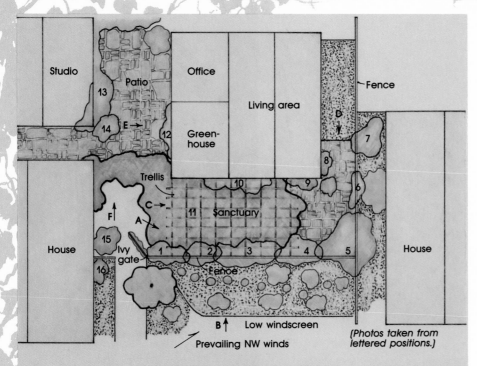

SANCTUARY VINES AND FRIENDS

Key	Common name (Botanical name)	Bloom time*	Flower color	Cold hardiness
1	Rose 'Cécile Brunner' (*Rosa* spp.)	Summer	Blush pink	
2	Hall's honeysuckle (*Lonicera japonica* 'Halliana')	Summer	Yellow and cream	-40°F
3	Cape honeysuckle (*Tecomaria capensis*)	Fall	Bright orange-red	20°F
4	Passionflower (*Passiflora Pfordtii*)	Summer	Purple and pink	
5	Silky wisteria (*Wisteria venusta* 'Alba')	Spring	White	-20°F
6	Anemone vine (*Clematis montana*)	Spring	Pale pink	-30°F
7	Echium [shrub] (*Echium vulgare*)	Summer	Purple	
8	Bower vine (*Pandorea jasminoides* 'Rosea')	Summer	Rose pink with dark throat	20°F
9	Argentine trumpet vine (*Clytostoma callistegioides*)	Summer	Pale violet	10°F
10	Fuchsias (*Fuschia* 'Voodoo', *F.* 'Swingtime')	Summer	Red and purple, red and white	
11	Grape 'Concord'	Fall	Fruit and foliage	
12	Boston ivy (*Parthenocissus tricuspidata*)		Foliage	-30°F
13	Pink jasmine (*Jasminum polyanthum*)	Spring to fall	White; pink buds	10°F
14	Glossy abelia [shrub] (*Abelia × grandiflora*)	Summer	Clusters of white flowers	-20°F
15	Viburnum [shrub] (*Viburnum japonicum*)		Foliage	0°F
16	Carolina jasmine (*Gelsemium sempervirens*)	Spring	Yellow	0°F

Time of bloom in author's Monterey, California, garden.

touching. First you must bow low (a humbling gesture) to move through the only break in a thick curtain of grape that covers the north end. Then you are at once confronted with large fronds of Australian tree ferns crossing the narrow path from either side, and before you make it to the center, long drooping stems of honeysuckle brush against your face.

The sanctuary is not colorful as gardens go. If anything, it tends to be a rather moody sort of place, sometimes somber under the fog and other times manic with dappled light. In its earliest years, a variety of annuals and perennials grew in the open sunny end, but today only forget-me-nots remain beneath a variety of foliage plants and hardy ferns. By and large, color is left to the vines.

The sanctuary's biggest show is in the spring, when the white silky wisteria (*Wisteria venusta* 'Alba') blooms. This lusty young nine-year-old will soon take over some of the sanctuary's canopy duty, and the long clusters of flowers will hang directly overhead. I'm training a younger Chinese wisteria (*W. sinensis*) with lavender blooms over the roof of the studio, and it should emerge into the patio area in another year or two. Anemone vine (*Clematis montana*) and the evergreen *Clematis Armandii* add some sprightly, light-pink and white flowers to spring.

The second act opens a short time later on the patio, when the exuberant pink jasmine (*Jasminum polyanthum*) bursts into clusters of fragrant tiny blooms, white with rose color on the outside of the throat. Masses of pink buds add a nice contrast. This evergreen may be the most vigorous and strongest climber (to 20 ft.) of the jasmines. Clipping and shaping are often suggested to control this species, but it's really quite an exquisite vine when allowed to grow with some degree of freedom, its thin stems and finely divided leaflets hanging gracefully or spraying about at the top in all directions.

By summer, flowers are scattered about like flecks of color in a cubic mead. Fuchsias, woven with asparagus fern (*Asparagus plumosus*), produce the boldest color, while the Argentine trumpet vine (*Clytostoma callistegioides*) provides pale-violet trumpets. The bower vine (*Pandorea jasminoides* 'Rosea') will most likely steal the show over the next couple of years. When it was rescued from miscalculated conditions in a friend's garden and transplanted to a south wall of the sanctuary, its leaves dropped at once and the creature sat barren for nearly two months before putting out new growth. By fall, the vine had recovered with a healthy rush, and even sent up a few of its beautiful trumpets, rose pink with dark throats.

When I transplant a vine, I expect it to lose most or even all of its leaves. But I

Illustration: Laura B. Goodwin and Susan Collins

don't give up on it easily. The old adage about a vine—"The first year it sleeps, the second year it creeps, the third year it leaps"—is simplistic, but useful. A vine will take whatever time is necessary to establish its roots and get a good footing before its aerial parts develop. Normally—if there is such a botanical term as "normally"—vines take one to three years to anchor their roots sufficiently before venturing far into the visible world.

With the contractions of autumn, Cape honeysuckle (*Tecomaria capensis*) comes into bloom, its brilliant orange-red flowers rising from the stem tips like a fountain. As a coarse barrier, tecomaria comes well recommended—it takes sun, heat, wind, salt air and some drought when established. To more thoroughly block winds, however, I grow a variety of ivies against the same trellis beneath the tecomaria leaves, as well as behind nearly all the vines that make up the front wall.

Into autumn, the sanctuary begins to reveal the bare bones that underlie the structure of it all. Exuberance gives way to senescence. Seeping in slowly, cooling down the thickness of summer, it brings to the gardener a deep-seated sense of his own role in nature and the obligations of all life to return itself to the next generation. By September, the vines have overgrown their space and become insanely intertwined; by October, the romance is over and they are ready to be disengaged.

Then comes most of the pruning; and this garden requires a great deal. But, as they say, "No cuts, no glory." I recycle much of the debris. Large leaves like the grape are directed to compost, but there is an abundant supply of smaller leaves to spread throughout the beds, providing a royal layer of winter mulch. I have never understood the advice to "clean up" at this time of year; it seems to me the perfect time to assign litter where it will do the most good. Having built up a sandy loam over the years with compost and mulch, I wish to keep life in the soil humming.

Some gardeners have a rose addiction, some get funny in the head over hedges. I have a vine habit. It's just one of those personal affairs that defies reason, but for me it offers an unusual view of studied negligence. In a garden, vines sit somewhere between manicured and untrammeled nature. They are a constant reminder that a garden is not a thing but an organic and psychological process. They provide a coarse-grained fabric that suits their gardener, who sports something of a natty herringbone personality himself. After all, gardening is foremost an outlet for the peculiarities of one's temperament. It's the freest space we have today. □

Mose Fadeem takes sanctuary in Monterey Bay, California, where he hosts "The Fanatic Gardener" on radio KAZU.

The profuse white flowers of silky wisteria and the pale-pink flowers of anemone vine dominate a corner of the sanctuary in early spring. (D)

Framed by Boston ivy, the cane begonia 'Irene Nuss' is visible through a window of the author's greenhouse. (E)

Grape leaves cover much of the sanctuary and here form a low arch next to the house. (F)

A Front-Yard Makeover
Good fences make good neighbors

by Michael Glassman

Ever since ornamental landscapes replaced front-yard fruit and vegetable patches in the early 19th century, the typical American front yard has functioned like an old-fashioned parlor—a place to show off to guests, admired but seldom used by the family. Nowadays, when homeowners frequently pay more for less living area both indoors and out, they

In the makeover of his clients' front yard, landscape designer Glassman transformed part of their former lawn into a private, yet inviting, courtyard enclosed by a fence (above). The wide brick walkway leads visitors from the street through the front gates, and also serves as a mini-patio. The narrower walkway leads to the driveway.

want more from their front yards. During the past 13 years as a landscape designer and installer in California, I've helped dozens of homeowners change their sterile front yards into peaceful, plant-filled retreats and places for entertaining. Outdoor living is pleasant practically year round in our mild climate, but even in colder climates, such outdoor rooms can be enjoyed for four or five months each year.

Most of my clients have the same goals, and the same concerns, in mind when they undertake a front-yard makeover. They want the private feeling of a room, but they don't want to feel confined. Getting the right balance between privacy and openness, security and welcome is challenging. The design must also be attractive and complement the architecture of the house and the character of the existing landscape. My solutions

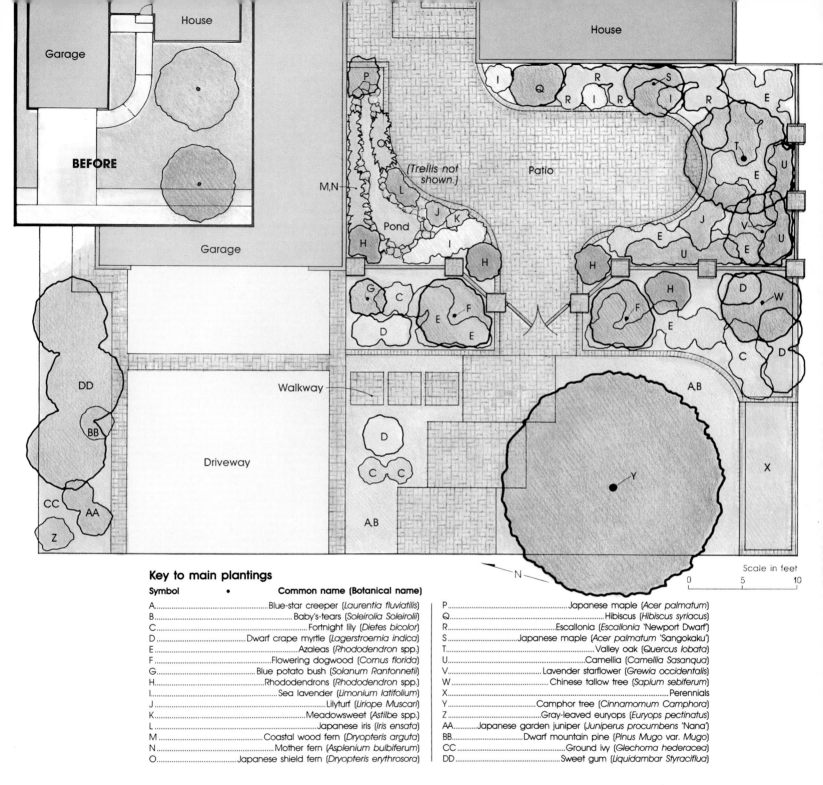

Key to main plantings

Symbol	•	Common name (Botanical name)
A		Blue-star creeper (*Laurentia fluviatilis*)
B		Baby's-tears (*Soleirolia Soleirolii*)
C		Fortnight lily (*Dietes bicolor*)
D		Dwarf crape myrtle (*Lagerstroemia indica*)
E		Azaleas (*Rhododendron* spp.)
F		Flowering dogwood (*Cornus florida*)
G		Blue potato bush (*Solanum Rantonnetii*)
H		Rhododendrons (*Rhododendron* spp.)
I		Sea lavender (*Limonium latifolium*)
J		Lilyturf (*Liriope Muscari*)
K		Meadowsweet (*Astilbe* spp.)
L		Japanese iris (*Iris ensata*)
M		Coastal wood fern (*Dryopteris arguta*)
N		Mother fern (*Asplenium bulbiferum*)
O		Japanese shield fern (*Dryopteris erythrosora*)
P		Japanese maple (*Acer palmatum*)
Q		Hibiscus (*Hibiscus syriacus*)
R		Escallonia (*Escallonia* 'Newport Dwarf')
S		Japanese maple (*Acer palmatum* 'Sangokaku')
T		Valley oak (*Quercus lobata*)
U		Camellia (*Camellia Sasanqua*)
V		Lavender starflower (*Grewia occidentalis*)
W		Chinese tallow tree (*Sapium sebiferum*)
X		Perennials
Y		Camphor tree (*Cinnamomum Camphora*)
Z		Gray-leaved euryops (*Euryops pectinatus*)
AA		Japanese garden juniper (*Juniperus procumbens* 'Nana')
BB		Dwarf mountain pine (*Pinus Mugo* var. *Mugo*)
CC		Ground ivy (*Glechoma hederacea*)
DD		Sweet gum (*Liquidambar Styraciflua*)

involve creating enclosures — fences, walls and plantings in a variety of styles and configurations.

While an enclosure is often the best solution to a client's needs, it may run afoul of the community's rules. In many cities and counties, building codes or ordinances specify the minimum distance that fences or walls over a specified height must be set back from the street. Each locale has its own reasons for these laws — fire safety, aesthetics, motorists' visibility. Here in Sacramento, a 6-ft.-high fence must be at least 25 ft. from the street. Such requirements might seem to make it im-

possible to carve a usable private space out of many front yards, which extend only 30 ft. to 35 ft. back from the street. Generally, however, the codes permit the building of a low wall, fence or planter as far out as the property line, and make no restrictions on shrubs or trees. Any of these can form the framework for a secluded space. I've created entertainment areas with 3-ft.-high raised planters. Filled with tall shrubs and backed up by a dense planting of even taller shrubs, a low planter is an effective privacy screen. I've also planted a thick grove of evergreen trees or an evergreen hedge to en-

close an area. Planters and shrubs form an outdoor-cafe-like enclosure; a grove lends a rustic feeling, while a hedge is more formal.

When setback restrictions can be met, the majority of my clients prefer the greater security and privacy afforded by a fence or a wall. For me, the most stimulating part of these jobs is considering the many possibilities of style and shape. I make some of these screens entirely of stucco or brick, but I prefer wood, in combination with these materials or on its own. I like the way wood looks, and it's inexpensive here.

A case study

The best way to explain the problems and challenges of redesigning a front yard is by example. Three years ago, Illa and Don Collins asked me to help them with their yard. Although they liked their home and the surrounding older neighborhood in south Sacramento, they needed a private, outdoor entertainment area. They frequently socialize, often hosting large parties. Mrs. Collins, who is politically active, regularly holds fund raisers at home for 50 to 100 people. The backyard was already occupied by a dog, a goose, rabbits, children's toys and a vegetable garden, so we turned to the front yard.

The Collinses' ranch-style house, set back 45 ft. from the street, forms an L-shape with the adjacent garage. Brick wainscoting rings the lower part of the olive-green house; vertical wood siding covers the upper part and the entire garage. The overgrown foundation shrubs and 2,000-sq.-ft. front lawn, which extended to the street, were nothing more than a dismal appendage to the house. Connecting the garage and the street was a cracked, uneven, narrow concrete

The patio (above) provides ample room for entertaining guests and family relaxation. Decorative scrollwork on the upper part of the gates adds a Victorian touch. Straight ahead, an overhead trellis shades a fish pond and the ferns and baby's-tears growing next to the garage wall (left). The curves of the trellis match those of the brick-edged planter below it and mirror those of the beds opposite it.

driveway; a sidewalk curved from the driveway to the front door, providing the only access to the house. Close to the house, a 30-ft.-tall cherry tree obstructed a potentially generous-sized entertainment area there. Exposed to the west, much of the yard was hot and uncomfortable in the afternoon, although a portion was shaded by a camphor tree (*Cinnamomum Camphora*).

Though privacy was important, the Collinses didn't want to be separated from their surroundings or the summer breezes. Most of the longtime residents of this neighborhood know each other and often congregate outdoors in their front yards. The Collinses were anxious for the neighbors to continue these visits, so the new environment had to be inviting. They also envisioned many colorful flowers,

Raised planters edge the patio, seen here curving to the left of the gates. Under the yellow-green leaves of a Japanese maple, sea lavender blooms in May. Red-flowered azaleas, camellias, blue-star creeper and lilyturf fill the rest of the bed, providing color throughout the year. Maintenance is minimal—most of the yard is structure, rather than plants, and low-maintenance plants were chosen.

rhododendrons, azaleas and Japanese maples in a low-maintenance garden. An enlarged driveway, but one that wouldn't overpower the yard with concrete, was needed, along with a new walkway to take visitors from the street to the house. The Collinses liked the look of brick, and hoped that I could incorporate a hint of Victorian architecture into the design without it clashing with the ranch-style house.

The central feature of the design we agreed upon is a courtyard in front of the house. Since the house and garage walls already formed two sides of a rectangle, it made the most sense to finish the rectangle by building a fence. The fence starts at the corner of the garage and runs parallel to the front of the house, jog-

ging out in the middle to emphasize a double gate that's set back 25 ft. from the street to comply with the local ordinance. The fence turns back to the house along a path leading to the backyard.

On both sides of the fence, low planters contain perennials and shrubs. A brick patio occupies much of the area in the 765-sq.-ft. courtyard, and extends out the double gate to form a wide walkway to the street. Next to the garage, a small fish pond and plantings shaded by a redwood trellis are a pleasing focal point for the courtyard, especially cool and refreshing during the hot, dry summers. Water recirculating through a waterfall masks much of the street noise.

Brick unifies the whole design, echoing the wainscoting on the house and avoiding an added-on appearance. The fence columns, patio, walkways and raised planters are all made of brick identical to that on the house. The columns flanking the double gate highlight the courtyard entrance. We painted the wooden fence between the columns to match the house. The bottom half of the fence is made of 1x4s set at a 45° angle to form vertical

louvers, which blend with the vertical siding on the house. They screen the courtyard from passersby, but allow viewing outward from certain positions within the courtyard, and they let breezes pass through. A square-patterned lattice above adds an airy quality to this otherwise solid-looking fence. The gates are left open most of the time, inviting people into the courtyard.

The top edge of the trellis next to the garage and the planter below it mirror the curved edge of the planter on the opposite side of the courtyard, reminiscent of a yin-yang symbol. I think curves like these contrast attractively with the straight lines of the house, creating a more relaxed and intimate environment. Outside the fence, I gave the brick paths and planters simpler, geometric lines to match the house.

The courtyard accommodates large groups comfortably, and is also a place for the Collinses to relax alone and enjoy their garden sculpture. The path from the street to the front gates is wide enough for groups of people to easily stroll back and forth or stop and talk, which makes it ideal for handling spill-over at large parties.

Installing the landscape was relatively simple but time-consuming—full-time work for two months for my crew of three. To prepare the area, we removed the cherry tree, killed the lawn with herbicide and dug it out, jackhammered out the old driveway, and leveled the site. Then we built the fence as described in the sidebar at right.

Next we built the low brick walls that form the planters and help vary the elevation on an otherwise flat site. Inside the fence, the walls curve with the patio; outside, they're straight. The beds in between connect under the fence. We laid the walls one brick wide and up to six bricks high on a concrete foundation. An additional course of bricks, about 2 in. by 4 in. by 6 in., laid at 90° to the planting bed caps the wall, its 1-in. overhang emphasizing the edge of the bed. (We cut the 6-in. bricks from 8-inchers.)

Along the garage wall, we built the pond, about 8 ft. long and 4 ft. wide, and the waterfall. The pump and filter are hidden in the garage. The trellis above the pond is made of redwood 1x2s, 2x4s and 2x6s, painted the same color as the fence.

To lay the patio, we first leveled the soil. Then we laid the bricks in a 6-in. to 8-in. sand base, the depth needed to stabilize them on our expanding and contracting clay soil, and dry-mortared them in place. To add variety, we arranged the bricks in a basket-weave pattern. They require very little maintenance compared to a lawn—occasional sweeping keeps them clean. We built the walkways next, offsetting 9-ft. by 5½-ft. sections from the gates to the street. Smaller sections, 3 ft. square, join the walk to the driveway, which we relaid with a coarse aggregate concrete and bordered with brick. Decorative low-voltage brass lights illuminate the plantings and nighttime activities.

I selected low-maintenance plants of varied heights that wouldn't block the fence—lower-growing shrubs, herbaceous perennials, and a few trees, chosen from those with a lacy-leaved canopy or ones that could be easily pruned to a nearly bare trunk along the fence. Blue, lavender, pink and white flowers predominate, with some yellow and red for contrast. Before planting, we installed an overhead automatic sprinkler system—a necessity in our climate, where most of the annual rainfall of 16 in. to 24 in. comes during the cold, rainy winters.

Just inside the gate, we planted rhododendrons with an understory of azaleas (*Rhododendron* spp.). Next to these, lily-turf (*Liriope Muscari*), impatiens, begonias, azaleas and more rhododendrons

grow near a small valley oak (*Quercus lobata*). Behind the oak, camellias (*Camellia Sasanqua*) grow in front of the fence. A coral-bark Japanese maple (*Acer palmatum* 'Sangokaku'), a blue-flowered hibiscus (*Hibiscus syriacus*), sea lavender (*Limonium latifolium*) and escallonia (*Escallonia* 'Newport Dwarf') fill the bed in front of the house. Baby's-tears (*Soleirolia Soleirolii*) and blue-star creeper (*Laurentia fluviatilis*) grow as a ground cover in all the beds.

Behind the pond, next to the garage wall, we planted coastal wood ferns (*Dryopteris arguta*) and mother ferns (*Asplenium bulbiferum*), which thrive in the moist, shadier environment. Pink-flowered meadowsweet (*Astilbe* spp.), purple-flowered Japanese iris (*Iris ensata*) and purple-flowered sea lavender (*Limonium* spp.) grow around the rest of the pond.

In the shade of the camphor tree, we planted a dogwood (*Cornus florida*) on each side of the gate; both its spring blooms and its fall foliage color are favorites of the Collinses. Blue potato bush (*Solanum Rantonnetii*) pruned as a standard, azaleas, dwarf crape myrtles (*Lagerstroemia indica*) and fortnight lilies (*Dietes bicolor*) grow in the remainder of these beds, adding color later in the spring and in the summer. Blue-star creeper and baby's-tears form a lush carpet under the camphor tree. A Chinese tallow tree (*Sapium sebiferum*) adds height at the corner of the fence.

To prepare the soil for all the plants, we first chopped up the native soil with a pickax and then mixed in a trucked-in mix of 30% nitrolyzed redwood compost and 70% topsoil to improve the clay soil and add slow-release nutrients. As we planted, we added fertilizer: acid fertilizer for the azaleas, camellias and rhododendrons; Agriform, a slow-release 20-10-5 fertilizer, for the rest. Maintenance is easy—deep watering three times a week in the dry season to wet the soil 6 in. deep, fertilizing the azaleas and camellias before and after bloom and the other plants in the spring and the fall, and a little weeding and pruning.

The Collinses' new front yard is now their outdoor living room, protected and private, yet inviting. The makeover turned out just as we had planned. In the courtyard, pots of flowering plants add a homey touch to the couple's retreat. Visitors freely come and go through the front entry, enticed by the open gates and the shade of the camphor tree. Although the yard is a break from traditional landscaping notions, it's a welcome addition to the neighborhood. □

Michael Glassman is a landscape designer and contractor. He owns Environmental Creations, Inc., in Sacramento, California.

Building the fence

The Collinses' fence creates a room for outdoor living, transforming a conventional front yard into a private courtyard. We built a louvered and latticed fence from redwood, the least expensive and most available wood in California for outdoor construction. To blend with the architecture of the house, I chose brick columns rather than wooden posts to support the sections of the fence.

The yard was flat and relatively level, so we didn't need to excavate. We laid out the fence line and the location for the brick columns, starting from the corner of the garage, by marking the fence line on the ground with a chalkline and using stakes to mark the column locations.

To make footings for the columns, we hand-dug 24-in.-square by 18-in.-deep holes, then laid and compacted a 6-in. base of pea gravel. We laid four pieces of ⅜-in. rebar on top of the gravel to reinforce each footing, and filled the holes with concrete made with Sakrete masonry cement. (In areas where the ground freezes, the base of the footing should be placed below the frost line.) As the concrete set up, we inserted four 7-ft.-long pieces of rebar in the center of each footing, 6 in. apart, sinking them into the concrete but not into the gravel. The rebar would reinforce a concrete core poured into the center of each brick column. After allowing the footing to cure for a few days, we laid the brick columns. We laid six bricks, each roughly 2 in. by 4 in. by 8 in., to a course, surrounding the upright rebar and leaving a hollow core.

To allow us to fasten the fence sections to the columns, we mortared in J-bolts between courses at three heights. We used 6-in. bolts and left about 1½ in. of the threaded shanks sticking out from the columns. After the morter had cured for a day or two, we filled the center rebar core of each column with Sakrete, tamping it as we poured. (We left the concrete a little on the wet side so that it would be easier to pour.) To top off each column, we made a 21-in.-square cap of brick, using the 2-in. by 4-in. by 8-in. brick as well as brick we cut into smaller sizes.

We built the fence's framework in place, one section at a time. First, we attached a 2x4 plate to the J-bolts on each column, boring shallow oversize holes in the plate to recess the nuts. Then we cut the middle and bottom 2x4 rails to fit snugly between the plates, and toenailed them in place. We nailed the uppermost rail on top of the plates as a cap, butted up against the columns.

We filled in the lower part of the framework with 1x4 louvers set on an angle and the upper part with prefabricated lattice panels that we purchased. We positioned the louvers with diagonal spacers cut from 2x2s, then toenailed the louvers to the rails.

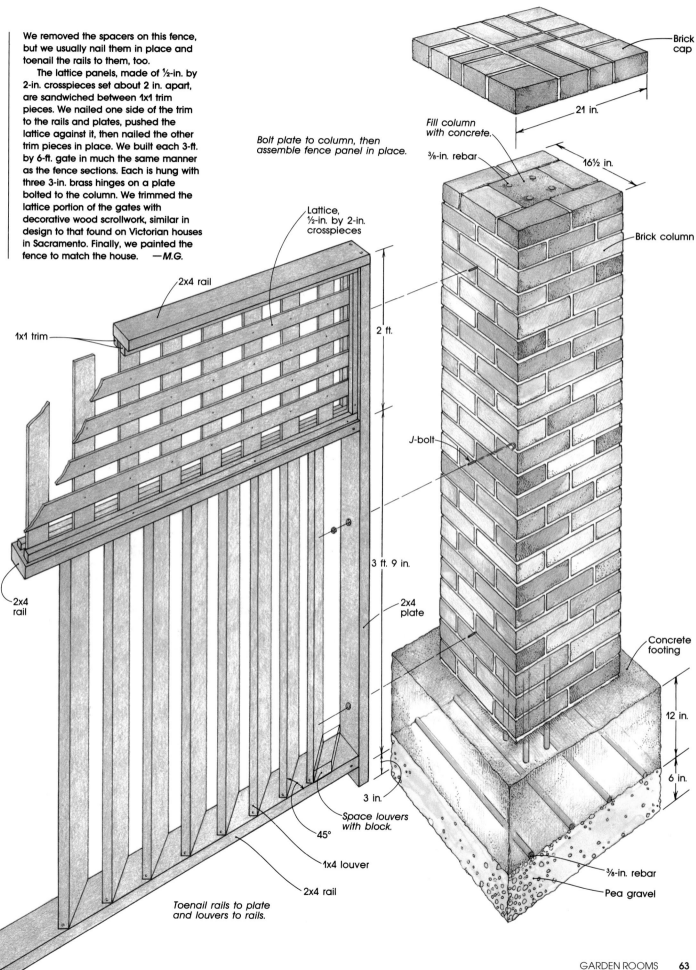

We removed the spacers on this fence, but we usually nail them in place and toenail the rails to them, too.

The lattice panels, made of ½-in. by 2-in. crosspieces set about 2 in. apart, are sandwiched between 1x1 trim pieces. We nailed one side of the trim to the rails and plates, pushed the lattice against it, then nailed the other trim pieces in place. We built each 3-ft. by 6-ft. gate in much the same manner as the fence sections. Each is hung with three 3-in. brass hinges on a plate bolted to the column. We trimmed the lattice portion of the gates with decorative wood scrollwork, similar in design to that found on Victorian houses in Sacramento. Finally, we painted the fence to match the house.   —M.G.

Brick cap

21 in.

Fill column with concrete.

16½ in.

⅜-in. rebar

Brick column

Bolt plate to column, then assemble fence panel in place.

Lattice, ½-in. by 2-in. crosspieces

2x4 rail

1x1 trim

2 ft.

J-bolt

2x4 rail

3 ft. 9 in.

2x4 plate

Concrete footing

12 in.

6 in.

3 in.

Space louvers with block.

45°

1x4 louver

2x4 rail

⅜-in. rebar

Pea gravel

Toenail rails to plate and louvers to rails.

A canopy of wisteria is framed by boxwood hedges, roses trained as standards and an orange tree heavy with fruit. The author's formal, hilltop garden in Oakland, California, overlooks a hidden informal garden. (Photo taken at A on site plan on p. 67.)

A Marriage of Garden Styles

Walks and waterways form the transition

by Barbara Lee

Like many gardeners, my husband, Larry, and I are attracted to both formal and informal styles of gar-

dens. But when the time came to build our garden, we had a hard time deciding which style to have. We solved our dilemma by choosing to have one of each. Then the challenge became how to create a smooth visual transition from a formal area to an informal one. The topography of our backyard garden helped us achieve our goal.

A good beginning

When we bought the house, we discovered terraces descending its sunny, west-facing backyard, each unseen from the ones above. We were overwhelmed by the beauty of the formal garden on the upper two levels. At the back door, for example, we were greeted by two large violet-

and pink-flowered Japanese wisterias cascading over a pergola, or trellis, and the roof of a garden house. The potential for creating an informal garden on the undeveloped levels below intrigued us, too.

We maintained the upper two levels as formal gardens. Gardens of this style are traditionally laid out symmetrically on either side of a central line, and they often display plants clipped in geometric shapes. This one was no exception. The top terrace was a 30-ft. deep by 60-ft. wide area. Rectangular, knee-high boxwood hedges surrounded two planting beds (see Site plan on p. 67). Straight brick paths ran between these beds, leading from the house to a brick patio at the edge of the terrace. Here the ancient Japanese wisteria that first attracted our attention covered a pergola above the patio (see photo on p. 64). Unhappily, the glass walls and fiberglass partitions that surrounded the patio, protecting it from wind, closed off spectacular views.

On the second terrace, 18 ft. deep by 60 ft. wide, we found four dwarf apple trees surrounded by more clipped boxwood hedges. The apple trees were underplanted with spring-flowering bulbs, all in full bloom.

We were content with the formal look of the top terrace, but we felt that the patio needed to be opened up to realize its full potential. So we decided early on to liberate the view from the top terrace (and don sweaters in the evening, if necessary). Without walls, the garden seems much larger, and the view provides a natural topic of conversation among guests.

The upper garden's neatly clipped formality, we discovered, ended abruptly at the 35-ft. deep by 60-ft. wide third terrace. Four fig trees, mottled with green and gray lichens, grew here. But here we also found unsightly clutter. Three wooden compost bins, a shed filled with scrap wood and two patches of bare dirt sat on either side of the brick path. We knew the grand sprawl of the fig trees would be a perfect foil for a naturally planted garden, once we cleared the clutter.

Eventually, we planned to create an informal garden for the third terrace. It would be a haven for quiet contemplation, once we muffled the wind with dense, naturalistic plantings and a waterfall. What a pleasant contrast to the formal look and social function of the upper two terraces.

Liberating the formal garden

The renovated 48-ft. by 60-ft. formal garden located on the top two terraces has an expansive, public feeling about it. Larry and I replaced the walls of the patio on the top terrace with redwood benches, which give us the seating we need to appreciate the wonderful view of the San Francisco Bay. The boundaries of the garden are visually extended by a borrowed landscape—the view of stately redwoods and Monterey pine trees growing on the surrounding properties.

We retained the existing hedges, annuals and perennials in the formal garden. The upper terrace is now carpeted with a rectangular, water-conserving fescue lawn. Each spring, I fill two of the three boxwood-bordered beds with tulips. In summer, I replace the tulips with zinnias, which give us

A ruby-hued Japanese maple is jeweled with droplets of water. Irises, Irish moss and English ivy weave a tapestry of texture beneath the gnarled limbs of a large fig tree. The fig, surrounded by shorter plants, gives the garden an illusion of greater depth. (Photo taken at B.)

The waterfall is a visual link between an upper, formal garden and a lower, informal garden. It flows from a small pool on the terrace above, over rock bluffs, through shallow pools, and then cascades into a pond on the third level. (Photo taken at C.)

Youthful plants promise color in the author's rock garden. From left, a Japanese maple, red-flowered azalea, magnolia, magenta-flowered hardy geranium and irises in bud rise behind blue-flowered ajuga, spiky fescue and rock-hugging sedums. (Photo taken at D.)

armloads of colorful cut flowers. The third bed is planted with a row of mature, shoulder-high, red- and pink-flowered rose bushes trained as standards (the lower stem of a standard is bare, and all of the leaves and flowers are concentrated in a formal ball shape at the top of the stem) (see photo on p. 64). These roses add height and color to the horizontal rows of clipped hedges. 'Double Delight', a hybrid tea rose, and 'Queen Elizabeth', a large-flowered grandiflora, are our particular favorites because they withstand diseases that are encouraged by our foggy summer mornings.

The formality of the upper garden is echoed in the second terrace by the row of dwarf apple trees and clipped boxwoods. We've kept both neatly pruned. A retaining wall at the back of the third terrace provides necessary support for the second.

Fashioning an informal garden

The informal garden is private, sheltering and quite different in its look from the upper two levels. We've laid the garden out asymmetrically, with curving walkways and individual plants that we've allowed to grow randomly. Here a tapestry of shape, texture and color is woven from informal groupings of the strap-like leaves of big, blue liriope (*Liriope muscari*) and mondo grass (*Ophiopogon* sp.), spreading sedums and hardy geraniums, and from broad-leaved and coniferous tall evergreens and Japanese maples.

A garden of our own creation replaces the compost bins and trees that once cluttered the third terrace. It took several years of growing vegetables and harvesting fruit from the trees, followed by many hours of canning, freezing and dehydrating for me to realize that I am a gardener, not a farmer. I also realized that I longed to hear the sound of running water. Larry and I thought that if we were to have water, we should also have a pond and some fish. So we removed two of the fig trees and put in a 5-ft. by 10-ft., free-form fiberglass pond where beans once grew. The 3-ft. deep pond protects the koi (fish that are related to goldfish) from marauding raccoons.

By replacing the redwood retaining wall and the straight brick walkways on this terrace with a stone wall and curving stone steps, we created natural-looking outcroppings, a waterfall and a stone-edged pond. Stone paths weave around the plants, revealing secret nooks.

We wanted to give visitors the feeling of being in a Japanese garden, which is the basic garden style from which informal gardens have evolved and a style that Larry and I admire. To do this, we kept the venerable fig tree and a trellised kiwi near the pond and added traditional Japanese garden plants like mugo pines and Japanese maples. This eclectic plant mix, along with the random stonework and curved lines, produces the look we were after.

The width of the terrace narrows to 15 ft. where the pond is located, but it seems much wider. Here I used a technique called forced perspective to give this impression. The fig tree, which is an immense plant growing very close to the edge of the third terrace, is backed by successively shorter plants. The diminishing sizes are exaggerated to give the illusion of greater distance when the plants are viewed either from the steps leading down from the second terrace above, or from either end of the third terrace (see photo on p. 65).

This garden is a private refuge from the chilly breezes that occasionally blow through the upper garden. Protected by terrace walls and trees, the informal garden is quiet and sunbaked. Here the only sounds are the soothing rush of falling water. The only sights are of the serene, naturally landscaped garden and the koi gliding silently beneath the surface of the pond. Coffee cup in hand, I often start my mornings here in quiet contemplation of the golden koi.

A smooth transition

Our biggest challenge in designing the informal garden was to find an appropriate way to seamlessly blend

Site plan

House

Wisteria-covered pergola

N

First terrace

Garden house

Patio

Second terrace

Third terrace

Retaining wall

Fig tree

Pond and waterfall

A B C D E

Pictures taken from lettered positions.

Pink-flowered hardy geraniums and mondo grass grow between stone steps in the informal garden. (Photo taken at E.)

the formal plantings, brick and geometric lines of the upper garden into the less formal stone and curved lines of the third terrace.

We found a wonderful stonemason, Bill Gorgas, whose years of renewing trails in Yosemite Park gave him an intimate knowledge of how stone looks in nature. He worked closely with us to create a transition between the two

gardens. Originally, brick steps led from the second to the third terrace. When we installed the informal garden, we wanted to blend the brick above into the stonework below. Bill found a way to make a smooth transition. He left the top two brick steps intact, because they are visible from the brick walkway on the second terrace. From that point on, however, he put in stepping stone stairs and a stone retaining wall for the third terrace. When we reach the stepping stones, our eyes are effortlessly drawn ahead along these natural materials toward the lower terrace.

A waterfall carries the eye—The waterfall, which flows from a small, stone-edged pool at the base of an apple tree on the second level down to the third level, is built into the retaining wall so that it looks as though it flows naturally over a rock bluff (see photo at top of facing page). The waterfall helps the eye move from the second to the third level and from the dry, upper gardens to the watery oasis below. The water flows through two waterfalls and small, shallow pools before it finally cascades gently into the koi pond.

From brick to stone—The cinder-block wall between the second and third terraces is now faced with carefully fitted rocks, continuing the transition from brick to stone (see photo, bottom of facing page). A second series of stone steps curves down from a brick path on the other side of the terrace. A Japanese maple, 'Sango Kaku', and an old dwarf pear tree punctuate a rock garden here, where more brick steps lead to an undeveloped fourth terrace.

I don't think I'll ever tire of improving our garden. I continually add new plants and move others. Every time we finish one project, we eagerly begin planning for the next one. ◼

Barbara Lee is a school principal and enjoys escaping into her Oakland, California, garden sanctuary.

Illustration: Rosalind L. Wanke

A Shared Garden

Tenants reclaim an apartment courtyard

by Rob Proctor

The Capitol Hill neighborhood near downtown Denver was on the decline when I moved there in 1981 and rented a Victorian rowhouse apartment. Dating to the 1890s, the building had a humble charm, but it had been sadly neglected. Inside, crusted paint buried the gorgeous wood moldings on my fireplace mantle; outside, only an ancient lilac, some English ivy and a clump of rhubarb survived to hint that the weed-choked courtyard out back had once been a garden.

The courtyard, about 40 ft. by 60 ft., is bordered by the two-story brick rowhouse building on the west and north sides, and by a one-story brick garage building on the east. A big box elder tree marks the south end and separates it from the lot next door. Although the courtyard adjoins the covered back porches and alcoves of the 12 rowhouse apartments, nobody used to spend much time out there. Baking between plain brick walls held little attraction. But one day, my friend David Macke and I decided to clear the weeds from beneath the box elder. Then he suggested that we might set out a few impatiens under the tree.

That was the turning point, initiating a great deal of gardening over the years. Now we plant 70 or more flats of impatiens and other transplants each year. The courtyard has been transformed from a barren wasteland to a colorful, flowery oasis, the focus of summer living. While David and I have done most of the designing and plant selection, other residents have helped in many ways, and the process of creating a garden has forged friendships among us. This garden is unusual because it isn't owned by the people who contribute to it and enjoy it. But some tenants have lived here a long time (20 years is the record), and even if we don't own the land, we benefit from the improvements. In fact, the story of the garden parallels the revitalization of the neighborhood.

The winter after we set out those first impatiens, I delved into the library at the Denver Botanic Gardens, studied stacks of seed catalogs, and drew and redrew plans. Before the earth had thawed, most of the neighbors had been drawn into the new project. The plan looked simple on paper: a large lawn for picnics and sunbathing, surrounded by gently curving perennial beds. Under the shade of the box elder we'd have a flagstone patio for reading and conversation. A second, larger patio would extend into the lawn. One resident, who's an architect, designed two simple wooden arbors for grapes and wisteria. We'd plant more vines to moderate the heat radiated from the brick walls. There would be colorful, fragrant flowers, including roses—an absolute necessity, everyone agreed. And, oh yes, we should check with the landlord. By coincidence, new owners had just inherited the building. They invested in a facelift for its exterior at the same time that we set to work on the garden. (They've been so pleased with this garden that they had me design a garden for their own home.)

The next few months were a frenzy of activity. Many tenants took part in the hard work of cleaning up and preparing the site. We spent two weekends cutting down a diseased elm tree one limb at a time, chopping the wood into smaller pieces and carting it off to the landfill. We sledgehammered out a crumbling concrete sidewalk and replaced it with a brick path. Since we also planned to edge the new beds with brick, scrounging for them became a neighborhood pastime. One neighbor had such a talent for brick-hunting that he ruined the suspension of his car. Other tenants helped purchase and transport flagstones for the patio, lumber for the arbors, flowerpots and other containers, and the benches and garden ornaments.

As we dug the beds, we excavated a number of objects from the heavily compacted clay soil in the courtyard. Most memorable were the clothesline-pole anchors. After removing one pair of iron clothesline poles, we were dismayed to discover the remains of 12 sets of wooden

predecessors. Apparently as each set of wooden poles had rotted, new ones had been installed, each mounted in concrete. One particularly obstinate chunk of concrete had me flat on my stomach with half my body down the hole, digging to find the bottom (or China, whichever came first). I began to wonder just how heavy laundry must have been in the old days to require such anchoring—5 ft. deep seemed a bit extreme.

But removing all the concrete was a blessing in disguise. It forced us to dig deeper than we had ever intended and gave us the opportunity to work in large quantities of bagged steer manure. As we were digging, we decided to move a rose-of-Sharon that one tenant had planted in a burst of springtime enthusiasm five years before. It was still scarcely a foot tall. We discovered the reason for its sluggish growth—another slab of cement lay 6 in. below the soil surface. When we relocated the poor plant in deep, rich soil, it responded by growing to 15 ft. in five years, the branches weighed down each year with double lavender blossoms.

We didn't do anything to the lawn until after we had started to plant the surrounding beds. Then we were hesitant to use an herbicide, because of the risk that it might drift, so we embarked on a program of hand-weeding to eliminate the crabgrass, dandelions and other weeds that half-filled the lawn. That was a lot of work during the first year, but we haven't had too much trouble keeping weeds out by hand since then. We fertilize the lawn each spring and fall, and give it a deep watering once a week in the summer. With this encouragement, the existing Kentucky bluegrass has filled in to make a nice turf.

We laid out a formal design for the garden, but within the planting beds the effect is very informal. I avoid the stiff, symmetrical patterns of Victorian carpet beds, and strive for a cottage-garden effect. The beds are lush, abundant and slightly overgrown, with colors and textures all intermingled in a way that looks random (although it's carefully planned). This style suits the setting, because it represents the

Tenants pitched in to build
the arbors. They scrounged
bricks to make paths
and border edgings.

Flower beds include the tenants'
favorite plants. Annuals provide
variety and change from
year to year.

A one-story brick wall (not shown here)
encloses the courtyard on this side.

Lush, abundant plantings create
a cottage-garden effect, much
like what the original tenants
might have done 100 years ago.

Courtyard garden

Rob Proctor and his fellow tenants
worked together to turn a weed-
choked courtyard behind their
Victorian rowhouse into the quiet,
colorful oasis shown here in a
watercolor that Proctor, a
botanical illustrator, painted.

Illustrations: Rob Proctor

One tenant designed and built the wooden arbor shown here, which supports a vigorous grapevine. The arbor is flanked by roses: on the left is 'Crimson Glory'; on the right is 'Coral Dawn'. In the foreground, in a bed bordering the oval lawn, are pink impatiens, silvery lamb's-ears, blue campanulas, white yarrows and pink malvas.

kind of gardening that the building's original tenants might have done. It also suits today's tenants, because it's a style that accommodates a wide variety of plants. When we were planning the garden, some people asked for peonies, others wanted daffodils, and so on. I incorporated all their favorites into the beds, but I'll admit that the majority of the plants are my choices—I'm the kind of gardener who's always finding something new to try.

Primarily I think about the height, form, texture and color of the flowers when I'm positioning plants. But to tie it all together, I include plants valued for their foliage, such as dusty-miller, lamb's-ears, silver sage, bergenia and ferns. Of course, all the beds are displayed against the lawn, an island of green. And the Virginia creeper, wisteria and grapevines that we planted on the arbors and the building walls make a soft, green curtain behind the flowers.

The beds are planted intensively—I don't want any bare earth to show during the growing season. By trial and error, I've learned that I can space plants quite close together if their roots occupy different layers of the soil. The spring bulbs, for example, root much deeper than the annuals that I tuck in to complement, contrast and unify the perennials.

Primroses, tulips, daffodils and other early bloomers start the season. Monkshood, astilbes, columbines, peonies, coralbells and hardy geraniums peak in June. They set the stage for roses and lilies, some of the star performers in this garden. The diminutive 'Angel Face' is probably the most popular rose in the courtyard, appreciated for its heavy "old-rose" scent and its soft-lavender color. My own favorite is the old shrub rose 'Kathleen'. Its clusters of tiny shell-pink single blossoms are perfect companions for *Lilium candidum,* the Madonna lily.

Lilies are my obsession. I grow more than 300 varieties of named hybrids and species in a bed west of the courtyard, and have established large clumps of single varieties throughout the garden. The Aurelian hybrids, or trumpet lilies, are especially vigorous plants that do very well here, although their young shoots are vulnerable to hard, late frosts in April. 'Black Dragon' is an outrageous trumpet lily— our five-year-old clump bears several stems that reach 8 ft. tall. The flowers are white inside and chocolate-maroon on the outside, and waft sweet perfume over the entire garden in late July.

The Asiatic hybrid lilies are also well suited to Denver; they thrive in our cold, dry winters and hot, dry summers. Some

especially vigorous clones are the pale-apricot 'Chinook', intense mahogany-red 'Red Knight' and soft fawn-buff 'Doeskin'. If I had to select a favorite, the nod would have to go to 'Tiger Babies'. Its charming name fits its appearance—the pale-pink petals enclose a glowing peach center liberally sprinkled with brown spots. Its delicate beauty belies a constitution of iron.

Annuals provide color from midsummer steadily until frost. And they offer an easy way to provide variety and change from year to year, within the steady framework of woody plants and perennials. The only way we can afford to have as many annuals as we want is to grow some of them ourselves. We equipped three of the rowhouse basements with grow-lights. I fill flats with preformed plastic six-packs, sow a few seeds directly into each cell and later thin all but the strongest seedling. The two biggest crops are impatiens and nicotianas, but I also sow at least half a flat apiece of annual gaillardias, coreopsis, stocks, Swan River daisies, heliotropes, tassel flowers and many other uncommon but desirable annuals. I don't bother growing petunias, because they're so readily available at garden centers.

Old-fashioned annuals, rather than the modern "improved" hybrids, seem to fit in best. The nicotianas, or flowering tobaccos, are some of my favorites. Among these, *Nicotiana alata* 'Grandiflora' (sometimes listed in catalogs under the synonym *N. affinis*) has one of the most engaging perfumes in the entire plant world. Its white flowers are almost luminous at dusk. If you've spent even one summer evening in a garden filled with its heady fragrance, you have to include it forever. Hybrid nicotianas have lost the stature and most of the fragrance of their ancestors, but they are perhaps the most floriferous annual. The 'Nicki' series grows to about 2 ft. tall. 'Nicki Pink' is my favorite, and forms ethereal clouds of clear-pink flowers.

Nicotianas are easily grown from tiny seeds started in February or March, and they often self-sow in our garden. They're best in sun or partial sun; I find them slow to bloom and lax in habit without at least half a day's sun. Although the hybrids need no attention to seed removal, *N. alata* should be cut back to encourage more branching and new bloom. Don't make the mistake of cutting it back all at once, though, or you will sorely miss its fragrance for several weeks. A drift of nicotianas can draw together divergent clumps of daisies, lilies and perennial bachelor's-buttons, providing a note of consistency throughout the season. They can anchor a bed between the comings and goings of star-attraction perennials. They will last up to, and often beyond, the first frost.

I must admit that I have a long-standing affection for petunias. I know that many gardeners disdain them, because they're considered common and often are used unimaginatively. If petunias were rare, though, and commanded a high price, we'd all be clamoring for them. If you haven't tried 'Summer Madness', you might want to reconsider. It's the best petunia in the world, period. With its lovely pink flowers and deeper red veining, it's bright and refined at the same time. Christened as one of the first of the "floribunda" race, its medium-size flowers completely smother the foliage. After a few feeble attempts to perform the customary deadheading, I gave up, unable to find the spent blossoms beneath the fresh ones. It clearly needed no help from me, and flowered "madly" with no assistance.

Over 200 containers—hanging baskets, windowboxes, tubs and pots—are arranged on the windowsills, steps, walkways and patios (see photos, p. 73). Using lots of plants in containers adds life and color, and softens the appearance of the concrete sidewalk that extends all along the back of the building and into the alcoves behind each apartment. We add more pots each year. One neighbor scours the flea markets for containers,

A rose-of-Sharon bush (on the right) was one of the few shrubs present when work began on the court-yard garden. Transplanted and well cared for, it now thrives. One of the most popular flowers in the garden is Nicotiana alata 'Grandiflora' (at center). Its white blossoms open at dusk, releasing a heady sweet perfume that fills the garden. In the pot at left are the petunia 'Summer Madness' and a spike plant.

and we stalk the discount pottery outlets.

One tenant brings out a collection of potted plants that spend the winter in a south-facing glassed hallway at the elementary school where he teaches. (He claims that the exchange of carbon dioxide and oxygen between the plants and the children leads to better health for all.) Tender-leaved tropicals fill a lath shadehouse along his apartment, and a collection of cacti and succulents bakes in a warm sunny spot.

But most of the containers are seasonal, refilled each spring with a different combination of plants. Some of the smaller containers have just a single plant; larger pots have mixed plantings. The hanging baskets that line the covered porches look best if they're planted uniformly. Last year we chose 'Summer Madness' petunias and 'Sapphire' lobelias as the main components. Other container plantings were more haphazard, although those two varieties were interlaced into many of the pots to carry running ribbons of the same colors throughout most areas. We like to make what people in Colorado call "French gardens" (I don't know if people in France would call them that), where groups of annuals are stuffed mercilessly into a big pot so that they romp all over each other and tumble down the sides. The best French gardens bloom profusely all summer, with a combination of flower forms, colors and sizes. We put as many as eight or ten plants in a 10-in. pot, and they grow to overflow it. In addition to the annuals, we often use spike plants (*Dracaena indivisa*) for a center point and variegated vinca (*Vinca major*) to trail down over the sides.

Planting the containers each year is a major undertaking. We turn to it as soon as we've finished putting the annuals into the flower beds. We assemble all the leftover flats of seedlings, cans of potting soil and the containers, and work as a team. One person fills a container with soil, another chooses a group of plants and sets them in place, and then someone carries the container to its summer location and gives it a good watering.

Filling so many containers requires bushels of potting soil. We can't afford to buy all new soil each year, so we recycle the supply we accumulate by asking tenants to bring home a bag from the store now and then. After frost each fall, we empty all the containers and store them outdoors, upside down and protected from rain and snow. The contents go into metal garbage pails, and the old foliage and roots compost and enrich the soil mix. We supplement it with more compost and a few freshly purchased bags of soil each spring. Garden books warn that reusing potting soil risks a buildup of disease, but so far we haven't had any trouble.

Despite the vagaries of its climate, I think Colorado is a marvelous place to garden. Summers are hot and dry, with cool nights; winters are cold and dry. Sunshine is abundant and so is wind. The soil is alkaline clay. This may not sound like paradise, but the lack of moisture and humidity (annual precipitation is approximately 14 in.) prevents the rot, diseases and pests that plague gardens with more abundant rainfall.

Our activities, like those of gardeners everywhere, vary with the season. Springtime in Denver is unpredictable, if it comes at all. An occasional warm February afternoon tempts us out to poke around, but even crocuses and snowdrops don't stir until March. Finally, one day in May we'll wonder if it's still too early to set out the annuals. The next day we might worry that it's too late. Intense sun and drying winds can desiccate fragile seedlings in minutes. Even stocky transplants are at the mercy of exceptionally warm days and scarce rainfall early in the season. We pay close attention to watering and sheltering them in these conditions.

In the summer, we go through the garden several times a week to trim, prune and deadhead. This really isn't a chore, because we enjoy being in the garden so much. We watch for pests and diseases, and use least-toxic controls. Sulfur dustings combat mildew and fungus. Most insects receive a dousing of Dr. Bronner's peppermint oil soap, mixed ½ cup to a gallon of water. Outbreaks of aphids are hit with a blast of pyrethrum.

There's no built-in sprinkler system, so we have to water by hand with a hose. For the beds, which are mulched with cedar chips, one deep watering each week is sufficient, even in high heat. The containers, though, need water daily. Because of them, I can't take off during the summer unless I've lined up a reliable substitute waterer. Along with watering, we apply a balanced fertilizer to all the container-grown plants and garden several times during the season.

Fall cleanup in the garden is easy, since we do so little. We remove the annuals to a compost pile, except those that sometimes survive the winter, such as dusty-miller. We don't prune or cut down the perennials or shrubs, as the seedpods and bare branches provide winter interest. Roses are left unpruned, because the frosted foliage helps protect their vulnerable crowns during harsh winters without protective snow cover. After Christmas, we comb the alleys for discarded trees to chop up and spread on the beds. Then we withdraw from the garden until spring.

All the tenants enjoy the garden in the summer. We relax on the sunny lawn after work, or find refuge in the shade to read the newspaper. Barbecues and birthday parties are favorite occasions. Setting a VCR beneath one of the arbors creates an instant "drive-in movie"—although we must look pretty silly parked in our lawn chairs and wrapped in sweaters on a Saturday night. Each year, we throw an elaborate garden party to celebrate a different time of the season. One exalted "Tulipmania"; another, "The Colors of Summer." Preparations go on for weeks, as we order champagne for punch, get the tent and tablecloths, polish silver, and make elegant hors d'oeuvres. Several hundred guests attend our annual fete, and occasionally one will exclaim, "This looks just like my grandmother's garden!" Considering its humble beginnings, we consider that a high compliment indeed.

What began in the courtyard garden is now reshaping the neighborhood. We're working our way down the block. Three years ago, David and I bought and moved into the house next door. We tore down the privacy fence separating the two properties and added a new "room" to the garden. While they mingle into each other, each property features different groups and combinations of plants, and has a separate mood and personality.

Two years ago, we expanded into the weed-choked vacant lot that adjoins the house. It belongs to the church down the street, and had been a chainlink-fenced eyesore since the early 1960s when the old houses on it were demolished. This garden was an ambitious project, since the buildings had simply been bulldozed into the basements. I'm sure we could have reconstructed them from the debris we excavated. Members of the church, including the pastor and his wife, assisted with the original three-week "dig," contributed flowers from their own gardens and continue to provide weeding help. The "church garden" now has a formal herb garden (with, at its center, a cement pineapple to symbolize the neighborhood's unity and friendship), vegetable beds and encircling perennial borders enclosed by picket fences. We share the huge harvest of tomatoes, beans, peppers and squash with the entire block and the church's soup kitchen.

Now a task force has been created to dispose of the water-guzzling bluegrass planted in the area between curb and sidewalk and replace it with low-water xeriscape plantings on the entire side of this block. An unofficial flower-box competition motivates everyone to spruce up the front entryways each spring. The entire neighborhood has gotten into the spirit of gardening, and new flower beds are sprouting up and down the street. □

Rob Proctor's landscape watercolors and botanical drawings are featured in private collections across the country. He teaches at the Denver Botanic Gardens.

Pink 'Summer Madness' petunias and geraniums, red zinnias, yellow marigolds, spike plant, and trailing-vinca foliage.

Pink petunias, white balsam, silvery dusty-miller and blue lobelia.

White petunias, lobelia, dusty-miller, and spike-plant foliage.

Gardens in pots

More than 200 hanging baskets, windowboxes, flowerpots and other containers bring the garden right up to the walls of the rowhouse building. Proctor plants the containers in May with seedlings of annuals, which bloom until frost kills the plants, usually in October. 'Summer Madness' petunias, pink with red veins in the petals, and 'Sapphire' trailing blue lobelias are used repeatedly to unify the plantings, and other plants are chosen to add variety of color and form. The containers dry out quickly in Denver's sunny, arid climate. Proctor makes the rounds with a hose and waters them daily (above).

Pink and purple petunias, pink impatiens, coleus, white marguerites, yellow marigolds, basil, geraniums, white feverfew, and blue spiderwort.

Shaping a Garden
With Illusion
Tropical effects in a small space

by Barry Friesen

Garden-making often involves creating illusions. Careful choice and arrangement of plants and structures can make a small garden appear larger, suggest different levels on a flat site, evoke the feeling of a meadow in a suburban yard, or create a sense of privacy in a crowded neighborhood. The desire to transform what's there into something else is basic to much garden design. And when it's done well, make-believe in the garden seems real.

Knowing what illusion you want to create is often easy, but figuring out how to make it work within the limitations of a particular site can be a challenge. About ten years ago, I decided I wanted an expanse of tropical rain forest in my backyard. What I had to work with was a moderately sloped square approximately 50 ft. on a side, pocked by the remains of several structures—including a 1950s bomb shelter—and covered with a tangled mass of poison oak, blackberries and ivy. Located in northern California, the site got no rain during the summer. With some fairly simple design tricks and a good deal of work, however, I was able to give the place the feel, if not the substance, of a rain forest, and to make the small garden seem much larger without moving a lot of soil or spending lots of money. You could use these and similar ideas to create illusions in gardens of completely different character and size.

The prospects—Despite the unpromising description I've just given of the pre-rain-forest backyard, I actually traded houses with our neighbor to get it. My wife, Toni, and I had lived next door, and over several years I came to see the property's garden potential. Much of the yard is shaded by tall trees on the perimeter and a beautiful California live oak near the center. Most enticing was a creek that runs along the lower edge of the property. Full of water year round, it's the perfect setting for the moisture- and shade-loving plants I'm fond of.

Toni and I became captivated by tropical rain forests on our Hawaiian honeymoon. Day after day, we walked through the lush green foliage that stretched from the tree canopy down to the forest floor. In the partially shaded understory, large leaves of various textures and shades of green dominated, highlighted by variegated foliage and a sprinkling of spectacular flowers. A far cry from the ever-blooming, sunny borders we were accustomed to! Plants we'd never seen before twined up and down, enclosing us in cool pockets of vegetation. Tree ferns especially caught our eye, but the diversity among the different species was phenomenal. Water permeated natural and designed gardens alike, dripping from plants and flowing through creeks and waterfalls rimmed with lava rock. We often felt that we were miles from civilization, in a sort of wonderland retreat.

Of course, we couldn't duplicate this at home. We had a canopy of shade trees, but filling in between and beneath them with a solid mass of large-leaved plants would overwhelm the small yard and blur the distinction between the garden and its surroundings. Even though I could pump as much water as I wanted from the creek, I couldn't count on many of the Hawaiian plants we'd seen surviving our occasional freezes and low humidity.

The creek, though, would allow me to mimic the watery environment so important to the feel of the rain forest. I could use smaller plants tolerant of our conditions to create illusions of multilayered foliage. To encourage lush growth, I'd install an automatically controlled irrigation system that would completely cover the garden. While I was still in Hawaii, I sketched out a design for the garden, which I followed pretty closely during the five years it took to complete it.

The principles—Several devices give the impression that the garden is larger than it actually is. First, I decided to make all the elements of the garden small. My childhood memories of Disneyland, where everything is built slightly smaller than life size, convinced me that this would create the magical atmosphere I wanted. I built narrow paths and a tiny bridge barely wide enough for one person to cross. I used small- and medium-size plants rather than trees, choosing ones with more compact foliage and flowers than those of true rain-forest plants. My dwarf-conifer and bonsai collection blended in perfectly with these, as did many of the small plants I included for the plant-identification classes I used to teach.

Second, I divided the garden into three partially enclosed areas, like rooms—a gazebo, a patio and a waterfall pond (see the site plan on p. 76). I thought about designing the rooms in this garden in much the same way that I think of building rooms in a house, each with its own character and function. Breaking up a larger space into individual areas and revealing them one at a time gives the impression of greater space. From the deck and upper part of the garden, the waterfall pond can barely be seen, and the patio is totally hidden. Even the gazebo, the most exposed room, becomes invisible from the bottom of the slope. As landing places on the slope, all the rooms encourage visitors walking through the garden to stop and take in the details close at hand. The curving path of timber steps that connects the rooms also makes the garden seem larger. Each time it disappears around a bend, its destination is left to the imagination.

Finally, I exaggerated the lines of perspective from the principal vantage point, the deck. I gradually narrowed the steps as they wound downhill, increasing the viewer's normal sense that things get smaller as they get farther away. Placing plants with medium-size leaves closer to the top of the garden and those with smaller leaves at a distance had a similar effect.

Water, black lava rock and plants are the elements of the garden's tropical rain-forest look. The bomb shelter was a perfect location for a waterfall and pond, fed by a man-made creek meandering through the garden. Lava rock lines the waterways and edges of the paths, and serves as stepping-stones and the patio floor. Tree ferns and a few orchids are the only true rain-forest plants. A great many different plants with variegated, colored or textured foliage thrive here, and a continuous cover of these in many shades of green enhances the garden's lushness. Flowering plants add seasonal interest, and vines clamber up fences around the garden perimeter, rather than up trees as in the rain forest. The water and predominance of green lend a cool feeling to the garden. On the following four pages, the text and photos detail specific areas of the garden and the illusions in them.

Author Friesen created the illusion of a tropical rain forest in his small northern California backyard, while making the garden appear larger than it is. Viewed here from the living-room deck, a timber-step path leads downhill to a barely visible waterfall pond and loops around to other roomlike areas in the garden (facing page). A continuous cover of low-growing plants of different shades of green, linked by a carpet of baby's-tears, gives a tropical feeling while matching the garden's small scale. The delicate, colorful leaves of a red laceleaf Japanese maple (foreground) highlight the top of the path, and an Australian tree fern sits above the pond.

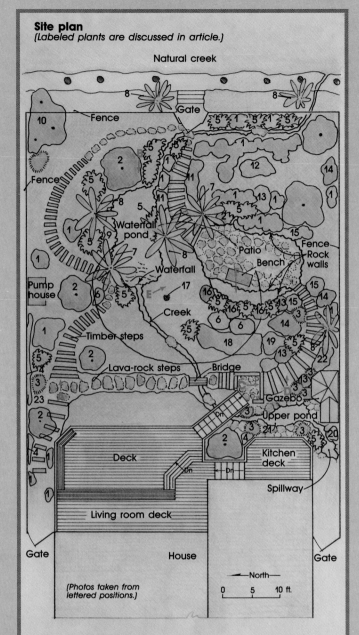

Site plan
(Labeled plants are discussed in article.)

Natural creek

Fence

Gate

10

Fence

2

Waterfall pond

Pump house

Waterfall

Creek

17

Timber steps

Lava-rock steps

Bridge

Patio

Bench

Fence

Rock walls

Gazebo

Upper pond

Spillway

Deck

Kitchen deck

Living room deck

Gate

House

Gate

(Photos taken from lettered positions.)

North

0   5   10 ft.

Key to plantings

Symbol • Common name (Botanical name)

1...............Azalea (*Rhododendron* cvs.)
2...............Japanese maple (*Acer palmatum* cvs.)
3...............Dwarf conifer spp.
4...............Vines
5...............Fern spp.
6...............Rhododendron (*Rhododendron* cvs.)
7...............Australian tree fern (*Alsophila Cooperi*)
8...............Tasmanian tree fern (*Dicksonia antarctica*)
9...............Grassy-leaved sweet flag (*Acorus gramineus* 'Variegatus')
10...............Azara (*Azara microphylla*)
11...............Chinese pieris (*Pieris Forrestii*)
12...............Cymbidium orchid (*Cymbidium* spp.)
13...............Strawberry geranium (*Saxifraga stolonifera*)
14...............Camellia (*Camellia japonica* cvs.)
15...............Mondo grass (*Ophiopogon japonicus*)
16...............Lily-of-the-valley bush (*Pieris japonica* 'Variegata')
17...............California live oak (*Quercus agrifolia*)
18...............Viburnum (*Viburnum Davidii*)
19...............Winter daphne (*Daphne odora* 'Marginata')
20...............Kaffir lily (*Clivia miniata*)
21...............Parrot's-feather (*Myriophyllum aquaticum*)
22...............Common periwinkle (*Vinca minor*)
23...............Baby's-tears (*Soleirolia Soleirolii*)

A section of path spanning the length of the garden on the north side disappears from view, adding dimension to the garden. To create an impression of greater distance, Friesen narrowed the timber steps from the top one (foreground) to the bottom one. He laid the timbers on level, tamped-down soil and anchored them with lengths of ⅜-in. rebar hammered through holes he drilled. (Photo taken at A on site plan.)

THE PATH
Shorter than it seems

The path loops around the garden. I wanted to emphasize the sections of the path running up and down the hill, so I made them of 6-in. by 8-in. pressure-treated timbers; those running across the hill are lava rock. The loop connects all the parts of the garden and enables me to poke around its nooks and crannies without constantly retracing my steps.

The timber steps get narrower as they descend the hill, from between 4 ft. and 5 ft. wide at the top to 2 ft. at the bottom. Likewise, I decreased the run slightly (the distance from the front to the back of the steps). This illusion works best when viewed from the deck or the top of the stairs, but I think it adds to the sense of magic in the garden even when it's not consciously perceived. Visitors often think the garden looks longer than it is wide, and are surprised when I tell them it's not.

The twists and turns of the path also make the garden look bigger by drawing the eye and the feet into the garden and revealing only a portion of the vista at a time. I think a curving path encourages exploration, which the garden rewards with the waterfall pond, patio and gazebo.

I wanted the curves to look pleasing, but not contrived, so I placed plants, big rocks or mounds of soil at the turns to provide a seemingly logical reason for the path's bending there. For example, at the first bow in the path on the north side of the garden, I planted a green-leaf Japanese maple (*Acer palmatum*) and a creamy yellow-flowered rhododendron (*Rhododendron racemosum* 'Saffron Queen') on one side, and an Australian tree fern (*Alsophila Cooperi*) on the other. Tree ferns alongside the long section of path at the bottom of the garden similarly divert its direction.

The waterfall pond is a room to view rather than enter (above). Ferns such as the Tasmanian tree fern (foreground, right) and the Australian tree fern (background, left) predominate, accented by colorful flowers and foliage. To transform the old bomb shelter (below) into the waterfall pond, Friesen installed back walls of reinforced concrete faced with lava rock, side walls of mortared-in lava rock, and a concrete floor. (Photos taken at B on site plan.)

A WATER ROOM
Tropical grotto in miniature

The watercourses in the garden capture the essence of the Hawaiian rain forest for me. In particular, I wanted the waterfall pond to look like a fern grotto I'd seen in Hawaii, with moss-covered rocks and plants spilling over its banks. The pond is a room to view from the surrounding path, rather than a room to enter.

Water runs from the house to the bottom of the hill. It travels from a small spillway near the kitchen into a little pond, empties into a narrow creek that flows under the deck stairs and a tiny bridge, and courses over the waterfall into a larger pond. Finally, it wends its way out of the garden and empties into the natural creek.

The waterways also serve as a drainage system for house and garden runoff. I ran all the house downspouts into an underground drainage pipe that empties into the spillway. Water that I've pumped up from the natural creek also flows out here. When it rains hard, water rushes through the system; I can also switch the pump on and off to create a flow.

I made the waterfall pond where the bomb shelter had stood. The hillside was already dug out, but I had to shore up the steep slope at the back and fashion rock-faced banks on the sides. I dug out the sides, then built an 8-ft.-tall reinforced-concrete retaining wall at the back and slightly shorter ones on the sides, facing all the walls with lava rock. The floor of the pond is reinforced concrete. I covered it with a layer of black-colored plaster shaped to eliminate sharp edges and make it look more natural.

I packed soil rather than mortar between some of the rocks in the side walls and planted ferns in it. I couldn't do the same in the back wall because

it required solid reinforcement. Instead, I kept these rocks constantly moist with daily watering from several sprinkler heads, and eventually moss spores blew in and took hold, covering the rocks there. At the edge of the pond, I made a small bed for marsh plants such as grassy-leaved sweet flag (*Acorus gramineus* 'Variegatus'). Because the bed is raised barely higher than the water level, it's almost invisible and the plants look as if they're growing up from the bottom of the pond.

A ROOM
WITH A VIEW
Gazebo lookout

The design of the gazebo, the upper pond and the surrounding plantings all reflect my attempt to keep the features of the garden small and in scale with each other. I wanted the gazebo to have an airy quality rather than an imposing one. Its asymmetrical shape and lightweight, open construction make it easy to walk in and out of and to look through. The bonsai plants displayed within it present an even more miniature world than that of the rest of the garden.

The plantings near the gazebo draw a viewer's eye down near the ground. Small-leaved perennial ground covers such as baby's-tears (*Soleirolia Soleirolii*), strawberry geraniums (*Saxifraga stolonifera*) and common periwinkle (*Vinca minor*), as well as low-growing plants, shift the viewer's perspective from the tall trees on the property line behind the gazebo to the smaller scale within the garden. The baby's-tears that covers much of the area is a volunteer, accidentally introduced into the garden with a container-grown plant. It flourished in the moist, shady environment. Although it overtook many of the ground covers I planted, I like the end result.

I incorporated some taller plants—tree ferns, rhododendrons, viburnums—to mimic the different levels of vegetation in a rain forest and to provide a transition to the tall trees around the perimeter of the garden. I made sure that their leaves and flowers weren't imposing. Some I grouped together and others I planted alone as focal points, like the bower vine (*Pandorea jasminoides*) climbing up the kitchen deck.

To increase the sense of depth in the garden, I frequently positioned plants with medium-size, more solid leaves in the foreground and ones with smaller, more delicately textured leaves behind. In the bottom photo at right, viewed from the gazebo, the medium-size leaves of camellia (*Camellia japonica*), rhododendron (*Rhododendron* 'Forsterianum') and winter daphne (*Daphne odora* 'Marginata') give way to the finely dissected leaves of Australian and Tasmanian tree ferns (*Alsophila Cooperi* and *Dicksonia antarctica*), and in the distance to the tiny leaves of azara shrubs (*Azara microphylla*).

Since I'm a plant collector at heart, I didn't follow many of the popular rules for unifying a garden: limiting the number of species, grouping many plants of one species or flower color together, or selecting plants for a succession of bloom. Although I wanted a cohesive-looking garden, I also wanted to display many different kinds of plants—I'd guess there are several hundred species here. The mat of baby's-tears helps unify the garden, even though I didn't plant it.

Rather than relying on plants to unify the garden, I counted on repeating built features to do so—the watercourses, the timber steps, the fence around the garden and the lava rock. The lava rock serves double-duty, evoking the feeling of the Hawaiian terrain as well. I hauled in about 10,000 lb. of it, both flat and rounder shapes. Lava rock is inexpensive and lightweight compared to fieldstone, and it looks quite attractive once it's blanketed with moss and ground covers.

A gazebo cantilevers over the slope like a bay window in a house (above), a perfect perch for viewing the garden. Low-growing plants such as the dwarf conifers, the parrot's-feather in the pond, the orange flowers of Kaffir lily and the tiny bonsai match the small scale of the garden, while the white-flowered bower vine adds a delicate highlight. Winding down from the gazebo, the path (below) leads to the patio sitting area, which is completely hidden by flowering shrubs from this vantage point. (Photos taken at C and D on site plan.)

Photo, top: Staff

A PRIVATE ROOM
Contemplative patio retreat

The patio sitting area provides privacy within the garden, a place to sit and contemplate the surroundings. I particularly enjoy this room. When I round the corner and it suddenly appears, I feel like I've discovered something special. And when I'm sitting within it, I feel immersed in a faraway tropical environment, although most of the plants enclosing it are quite commonly grown in northern California landscapes.

I chose the location for the patio in part because the slope flattened out there. I leveled an 8-ft. by 15-ft. terrace and paved it with flat lava rock, using the excess soil to form a bank on the downhill side. I shored up the slopes on both the uphill and downhill sides with a dry-laid lava-rock wall, 3 ft. to 4 ft. high—low enough so that I didn't worry about precise engineering. I packed soil in between the rocks behind the patio to make pockets for planting.

Plants with a variety of leaf textures, colors and shapes enclose the uphill side of the patio. Here, as in the rest of the garden, I relied on these subtle differences rather than splashy flowers or big plants as accents. Close to the ground, the heart-shaped, grayish veined leaves of strawberry geranium form an understory for three lily-of-the-valley bushes (*Pieris japonica* 'Variegata') planted alternately with an equal number of button ferns (*Pellaea rotundifolia*). The reddish cast of the new leaves of the lily-of-the-valley bush, along with its white, bell-shaped flowers, highlights the planting in early spring. Its oblong, cream-edged leaves contrast with the smaller, round, dark-green ones of the fern year round. The repeating sequence leads the eye from one end of the patio to the other, enhancing the sense of enclosure.

A pink-flowered camellia (*Camellia japonica*) and a fragrant, white-flowered rhododendron (*Rhododendron* 'Forsterianum') accent the area when they bloom in March and April (see bottom photo, facing page), and fade to a backdrop the rest of the year. The tiers of plants filter the sunlight, forming intriguing patterns within the room. Below the terrace, I planted lower-growing plants such as red-flowered azaleas (*Rhododendron* 'Hino Crimson'), mondo grass (*Ophiopogon japonicus*) and assorted ferns, leaving a "picture window" view of the lower part of the garden and the man-made and natural creek beyond.

Even though the leaves of all the plants surrounding the patio are much smaller than those I saw in the tropics, from a distance the solid green mass gives a similar impression. Shifting perspective to close range, the combination of leaf shapes, colors and textures adds an element of surprise even when the plants are not in bloom. ☐

Barry Friesen is a landscape and irrigation contractor in Berkeley, California.

Glimpsed from beneath the fronds of a Tasmanian tree fern, the patio sitting area looks like a secluded tropical retreat (above). From within this room, the view down to the natural creek extends the garden beyond the fence. Instead of relying on continuous bloom, Friesen mixed leaf shapes, textures and colors. Behind the patio (below), he grouped the heart-shaped leaves of strawberry geraniums, the oblong cream-edged leaves of lily-of-the-valley shrub, the round leaflets of button fern, and a white-flowered rhododendron. (Photos taken at E and F on site plan.)

Miniature landscape weds this house to its site. Dwarf plants and stone raised beds extend the architecture of the author's home. Naturally small conifers and Japanese maples repeat the subtle alpine appearance of the house.

A Miniature Mountain Landscape

Big boulders and small plants create an alpine vista

by Konrad Gauder

In 1982, my wife, Denise, and I moved into her childhood home. It was a run-down, Berkeley Craftsman-style house, vintage 1910. The house had been unoccupied for seven years, but it held out lots of promise. What garden there was consisted of a strip of Bermuda grass sloping to the street in front of the house. Old bottlebrush, hibiscus and an invasive flowering quince decorated the foundation. Overgrown roses gave an unkempt appearance to the narrow strip of side yard, and in back of the house was a poorly constructed concrete-brick patio surrounded by shrubbery, a Japanese maple, and plum and mulberry trees. We kept the maple.

Design goals

We decided to tackle the prospect of transforming the house and grounds ourselves. I had been designing and building gardens for several years, and Denise was studying to become a landscape architect. Our plan was to bring out the potential of the house by adding natural-looking redwood trim and siding, gently curved beams and well-proportioned detailing. Once the house was completed, it inspired us to create a garden that would reflect its new, alpine, chalet-like appearance. We wanted to integrate house and yard and to get away from the flatness of the city lot. We also wanted to create a miniature landscape to fit the scale of the small property (16 ft. x 40 ft. in front and 20 ft. x 40 ft. in back). At the same time, we hoped to make the space appear larger by choosing smaller-scale features, including plant and leaf sizes. Privacy and security from a busy city street were important. We also wanted to have a view of the rear garden from the house and sitting areas or outdoor rooms from which to enjoy the garden. Finally, we wanted it all to be low-maintenance.

An entry garden on a busy street

We designed a slightly formal entry garden with carefully joined stonework and neat, dwarf plants to enhance the house. The property sloped gently to the street and could have been retained with a rock garden, but too many dogs had easy access to the property for that delicate kind of garden to be safe. We decided, instead, to build low stone walls interconnecting large boulders placed along the

Privacy without blocking the light. A fence with a locking gate provides privacy and security for the side and back yards while the careful spacing of its posts allows light to stream through. An attached trellis supports the purple-flowering Chinese wisteria 'Cookes Purple'.

perimeter like precious stones in a necklace. These stone walls act as retaining walls for two raised beds, which now flank the driveway.

We decided the naturalistic style I had developed in my practice would perfectly suit our miniature landscape and keep it from looking contrived. As part of that style, we built rock outcroppings in front and back (more than 20 tons of boulders and 10 tons of smaller rocks were used) to create structural focal points around which to plant.

In the raised beds in front, around the carefully placed boulders, we planted well-behaved, naturally dwarf trees and conifers and low plants that would hug the rocks as in an alpine environment. These plants fit the scale of the landscape and require very little care.

Due to our closeness to a busy city street, privacy and security were also important in the front and side yards. But we also felt that openness and light were important. To meet both these needs, we settled on a gate and fence design that incorporated 2-in. spaces between vertical 2-in.-wide boards. It serves as a substantial barrier to the outside world while allowing ample light to enter.

The trellis above the entry gate has large timbers that mirror those used on the house. The sturdy proportions of the trellis give ample support to the Chinese wisteria vine (*Wisteria sinensis* 'Cookes Purple') we planted to climb upon it. We chose the wisteria for its purple color, as well as its tendency to bloom several times a year. Its moderate-sized leaves are in scale with its environment.

A mountainous vista in miniature

In the rear garden we wanted a full privacy barrier, but didn't want to block the light there, either. We chose a 6-ft.-tall board-and-batten fence topped with 18 in. of diagonal lath, which raises the height of the fence without blocking light.

The original back porch was in sad condition, so we demolished it and replaced it with a curvaceous, gracefully cantilevered deck. A built-in bench on the deck provides a great vantage point from which to view the garden.

To create a central brick patio surrounded by sloping, raised beds, we built low, concrete retaining walls around the perimeter of the property. The walls retain the raised beds and provide solid anchors for our fence posts, which we bolted to the walls on the outside. The fence totally hides the walls from our rear neighbors' view.

The boulders and retaining walls set the stage for the creation of a miniature amphitheater of planting beds, which eliminates the flatness of the city lot. By incorporating boulders, we reduced the amount of walking space, creating a sense of perspective as the eye travels micro distances. The effect is like viewing a mountain landscape in miniature.

Our plant materials suggest an alpine environment, yet maintain the scale and texture of a small garden. We chose trees and shrubs whose eventual size would not overwhelm and dwarf the garden, selecting them for their finely textured leaves or needles, their slow growth and their limited mature size.

Creating a low-maintenance garden

We live in drought-stricken California, so we grow trees, shrubs, hardy perennials and ground covers that do well with little water. We water only twice a week; an irrigation system makes the job easy and efficient. These same plants make for a low-maintenance garden—they require

A frame for the rear garden. An arch made of two posts with a curved lintel on top frames the entrance to the rear garden from the side yard. The arch stands at the far end of a path that meanders gently through the side yard. (*Photo taken at* **A** *on site plan, facing page.*)

A small-scale mountain landscape. The careful placement of rocks, water and plants recreates the feeling of a mountain landscape. Conifers, ornamental grasses, red Japanese maples and ground covers were all chosen for their small foliage and texture to reduce the scale of the panorama. At right, one of nature's pleasant surprises, a fern, is allowed to grow through a dwarf Japanese maple, creating a striking—but unplanned—composition. (*Photo taken at* **B** *on site plan, facing page.*)

Illustration, facing page: Denise Gauder

Photos taken at lettered positions. Front cover photo taken at **F**.

BUTTERFLY BUSH
MANZANITA 'DR HURD'
TANYOSHO PINE BLUE NORWAY SPRUCE
BELLFLOWER
WATERFALL
SEA THRIFT
MUGHO PINE JAPANESE MAPLE
BENCH

E

CARPET BUGLE
WATER WASH STEPPING STONES
POND

BENCH

WHITE PINE
BLUE OAT GRASS
WATER WASH STEPPING STONES
DECK
HERRINGBONE BRICK PATIO
D
LACE LEAF MAPLE
RIOTERA CYPRESS
DWARF HINOKI CYPRESS
DALMATION BELLFLOWER

CORAL BELLS
BOULDER

JAPANESE MAPLES
AZALEA
MONDO GRASS

BOULDERS (TYPICAL)

F

HEAVENLY BAMBOO

TEAK RAIL

C A B

BENCH

0   5   10

Scale, in feet

Plan view of backyard

N

Perennials and grasses create a harmonious composition that doesn't overwhelm the eye, but still appears colorful. Here, sprawling purple bellflower and grass-like sea thrift, with its small, pink flowers, combine with blue fescue, a lichen-covered rock and a curving patio edge to reinforce the natural effect. *(Photo taken at* **C** *on site plan p. 83.)*

little deadheading, clipping or dividing and no staking.

Conifers for structure—We selected a number of dwarf conifers for the structure their foliage creates throughout the year and to give the flavor of an alpine environment. One of the more striking cultivars selected for the rear garden is the dwarf Colorado blue spruce (*Picea pungens* 'Glauca Globosa'), distinctive for its low (18-in to 24-in.) growth and its fine texture as well as its striking gray-blue color. This plant, which grows only about one-half inch per year, contrasts wonderfully with bright greens and purples and can be used alone or in drifts that mass the color for a broader effect.

A pine tree whose name describes its appearance, the multi-branched Japanese umbrella pine (*Pinus densiflora* 'Umbraculifera'), occupies center stage in the rear garden, where it shelters the patio and provides handsome structure when viewed from the porch. With an expected mature height of 12 ft. to 15 ft., it won't dominate its limited space.

Various dwarf Hinoki cypress (*Chamaecyparis obtusa*) contribute their lush, needleless, whorled foliage in luscious colors from rich green to gold. Ranging from 2 ft. to 6 ft. in height, the cypresses offer us years of tidy, slow growth.

Deciduous trees for color—Complementing the conifers are deciduous trees, which provide dynamic color from spring's first blush through the brilliance of autumn. The foliage of a wonderful dwarf birch (*Betula alba* 'Trost's Dwarf') arches gracefully over a large vertical boulder. The tree's delicate texture and weeping habit complement the

rock and contrast with the house's natural-wood siding.

I had collected at least eight different varieties of Japanese maple (*Acer palmatum*) over the years, and I decided to place them in the planting palette. We put the larger ones next to large rocks in the backyard and nestled the smaller ones next to the brick stairway beside the entry gate to the side yard.

Broad-leaved evergreens—Among my favorite large shrubs is manzanita, noted for its sinewy, burgundy, smooth limbs and trunks, as well as its small, oval, gray to bright green leaves and inverted, pale pink, urn-like flowers, which appear in late January through early February here. I placed a Sonoma manzanita (*Arctostaphylos densiflora* 'Dr. Hurd'), an unusually water-tolerant cultivar with medium growth potential, in the back garden. Its position behind two closely spaced blue spruces allows the spruces' color to perfectly frame its smooth burgundy trunks and bright green foliage.

Perennials—Some perennial plants, such as lavender cotton (*Santolina chamaecyparissus*) we picked for foliage color. We clip the lavender cotton and allow it to hug the rocks. Its striking gray foliage cools the eye in the bright southern exposures in which it thrives and contrasts well with greens and purples.

Two durable, dependable, shade-tolerant, easy-maintenance, low-growing perennials—purple-flowering bellflower (*Campanula muralis*) and sea thrift (*Armeria maritima*)—add neat, self-contained foliage and wonderful flower colors that don't overwhelm the eye. The sea thrift is notable for its peak displays of pink, ball-like flowers on graceful stems. Several varieties of creeping thyme contribute their rock-embracing tendencies to the garden and provide a wonderful variety of colors—silvery gray to golden yellow foliage and white to lavender blossoms.

One of the real surprises was dwarf germander (*Teucrium chamaedrys* 'Prostratum'), whose habit of running underground without being invasive was a delightful discovery. It grows between rocks, while avoiding more open areas. This fine-textured, beautiful plant requires no clipping and, therefore, little maintenance.

Pink-flowering alpine geranium (*Erodium chamaedryoides*) and blue-flowered carpet bugleweed (*Ajuga reptans*) contribute color and durability to the shady areas. Alpine geranium blooms from spring to fall while remaining compact and non-invasive. This green-leaved bugleweed provides a bright accent among rocks and sends up 3-in.

flower spikes in the spring. Its foliage forms a neat 1-in. tall mat.

Ornamental grasses—To provide a vertical element and simulate the profuse growth of grasses in mountain areas, we planted ornamental grasses, most notably *Helictotrichon sempervirens* and blue fescue (*Festuca ovina* 'Glauca') and green fescue (*F amethystina*). We placed them next to vertical rocks, in drifts on slopes and under taller trees.

The grasses are as easy to maintain as the rest of the garden. Both the 3-ft. tall helictotrichon and the 6-in. to 12-in. tall fescues require only a trim in the late fall or early spring to rid them of dead leaves. In addition, their fine textures and handsome colors allow us to use them as interesting color accents—i.e., green fescue planted under blue spruce.

An alpine water feature—More than a year after the completion of the garden we decided to add a water feature to the northeast corner of the rear garden. It would provide further privacy by drowning out city noises while adding the tranquil feeling of a mountain stream and a place of rest.

We created an upper falls area and small pond, a gurgling stream bed and a lower cascade with a strong, recirculating waterfall. A large boulder was imposed in the space where we intended to build the lower pond. Rather than try to move it, we incorporated it into the composition. We placed stones into a concrete shell to form the falls and beside it to frame the cascade.

The garden and its stream have been a favorite play area for our two young daughters who have grown up scampering on the rocks, splashing in the water and spinning fantasies under the trees. In the course of routine weeding or pruning, I periodically encounter miniature kingdoms among the rocks and beneath shrubs, encampments of tiny Indians or groups of wild tigers and bears, even giraffes and elephants, hidden in the underbrush.

Our garden has become a place of peace and repose, a resting spot where the hurried and troubled pace of life outside can be set aside and inner thoughts and dreams can be realized. □

Konrad Gauder is a landscape designer in Berkeley, California, who specializes in the use of rocks in the landscape.

A tranquil mountain stream. Water rushes past rocks and boulders and emerges in a small pond, creating a tranquil sound that drowns out city noise. The sword-shaped leaves of Siberian iris fan out from behind a tall boulder and provide a vertical accent. (*Photo taken at **D** on site plan, p. 83.*)

A comfortable perch for enjoying the garden. A built-in bench on the back porch provides a vantage point from which to observe the garden. Some of the plantings were placed specifically to create a beautiful view from the porch. (*Photo taken at **E** on site plan, p. 83.*)

A moon gate offers glimpses of a perennial border and an open back yard. Though small, the author's property offers vistas, eye-catching structures and several distinct gardens—some of his requirements for a pleasing design. (Photo taken at A on the site plan on p. 89.)

All photos: David McDonald

Accents Make a Garden

Patio, vista, pond and plantings transform a city lot

by Douglas Bayley

Over the years, I have developed an idea of the perfect garden. There are certain essentials. One is a central open space with some classic feature such as an arbor or a tree. There should also be separate, densely planted gardens, each with a different theme. And I want a gate, a vista ending with a bench or tree or arbor that draws the eye, intersecting paths, the sudden glimpse of a view, a pond with the sound of splashing water and windblown ornamental grasses. Most important is a place to sit privately, alone or with family and friends.

You don't need a huge property for my ideal garden; I have all its elements in an 85-ft. × 45-ft. corner lot in Seattle. The front yard slopes steeply up from the street to the house, which sits close to the property line on one side. A path leads along the other side of the house to a level backyard. Front, side and back yards are organized and planted differently, and each contributes at least one of my ideal features (see site plan on p. 89).

Structures shape the garden

In a small garden, structures play a big role. Without taking up a lot of room, they can give plants a vertical place to grow, they can make focal points, and they can divide the property so the whole garden is not visible at a glance. In my garden, a wooden fence along the side street provides both privacy and a support for vines. It is echoed on the opposite side of the yard by a trellis that encloses a patio. A moon gate (so called because the open circle formed by the curve of the gate and the arch above it resembles a big, full moon) separates the

Graceful, arching clumps of the ornamental grass *Miscanthus sinensis* 'Gracillimus' dominate the steep front yard. (Photo taken at B.)

front yard from the side yard and acts as a focal point from two directions. Heavy timbers delineate planting beds and form steps. A simple rectangular pool repeats the shape of the patio and the adjacent back lawn.

From the start, I wanted a water feature. I felt that a formal shape would be the easiest to install and maintain. I also knew my wife and I would someday have small children and then I could convert the pool into a sandbox

A white bench in a private corner invites visitors to sit. Flanked by 'Skyrocket' junipers, the bench looks out on a vista across the backyard to a pool and patio. The gold-margined leaves of hostas brighten the bed beside the fence. (Photo taken at C.)

for a few years. I built the pool from timbers, waterproofed it with a plastic liner and added a small fountain to provide the soothing sound of moving water. The pool's formal shape is softened by the huge, roughly textured leaves of a moisture-loving *Gunnera manicata*. The area around the pool is densely planted, adding to the sense of escape when we retreat to the patio.

Creating focal points

When my wife and I moved in, most of the backyard was taken up by a driveway and garage. The aging concrete of the driveway came up easily. I turned the soil and amended it, and the area became a rectangular lawn, surrounded by planting beds. We kept the concrete pad that was the garage floor—it's now our patio.

At one end of the driveway-turned-lawn, against the fence, I made a focal point that caps the view from the patio across the longest vista on the property. A white wooden bench sits between two columnar 'Skyrocket' junipers with boxwood at their feet (see photo above). The effect is some-

what grand and formal for a modest garden, reminiscent of crisp, white summer houses in Maine.

When visitors come through the back gate, they enter the backyard near the bench. Now the other end of the yard becomes a distant vista, so I made a trellis over the patio for a focal point. The trellis had to support a wisteria, so I made it tall and sturdy—full-grown plants can consume and demolish structures that appear quite adequate when vines are new.

Some of my other ideas for focal points turned out to be misguided. For example, the first gate the carpenter mocked up at my direction was way too big. We came up with a smaller, lighter gate (the moon gate pictured on p. 86) which fits the style and size of the house much better. This gate provides another focal point and keeps young children and the dog safely inside the backyard.

Lots of plants in little space

Structures and focal points are important, but I love plants, too. I was determined to fit as many different kinds

as possible into my small space. So I created three separate theme gardens, one in the back, one along the side and one down the front slope.

A long, narrow border, edged by 6-in. timbers, runs along the lawn and behind the pond, across the back property line. Since the border is visible all year long, I used a mix of evergreen and deciduous plants. I also tried some bold textures and colored foliage. To echo the neighbor's row of purple-leaved cherry trees, I planted purple smokebush (*Cotinus coggygria* 'Purpureus'), a 'Sherwood Flame' Japanese maple and a dark-leaved black snakeroot (*Cimicifuga racemosa* 'Brunette'). The purple leaves mingle with dwarf conifers and colorful summer perennials and annuals.

The garden along the side of the house has a different theme. It is a double border that resembles a traditional English rose garden. Among the roses, I interplanted all the common plants I remember from childhood gardens: columbines, irises, peonies, salvias and hardy geraniums. The side garden is deciduous, except for sheared boxwoods in the corners, which gain prominence in winter. Color starts in spring with tulips and ends in October with Japanese anemones. I like to cut this garden back in the fall. It seems a luxury to have an area that can be entirely bare in the winter.

Grasses on a public corner

The house is on a corner, so the front has two sides with road frontage. It's a fairly busy corner for pedestrians, with three schools nearby and many children. It was an education to work in plain view on the street. People stopped to ask the names of plants, and tearing out plants and adding new ones became a way to meet the neighbors.

The front yard slopes steeply down to the sidewalk. The bank is sandy and exposed to full sun, so I used drought-tolerant, sun-loving plants and experimented with some ornamental grasses. I wanted to have strong seasonal change and evergreen plants, because the corner is on view all year.

I planted a mix of grasses and perennials plus deciduous and evergreen shrubs. The evergreens are ceanothus, a shrub with lilac-blue spring flowers; *Osmarea burkwoodii*, with fragrant spring flowers; and a few mugho pines. The biggest grass is vase-shaped *Miscanthus sinensis* 'Gracillimus'. I repeated clusters of plants with distinctive leaves and leaf colors: the blue-green grass *Helictotrichon sempervirens*; gray-green, fleshy-leaved *Sedum spectabile*; finely cut, silvery *Artemisia* 'Powis Castle', and gray-green sages. For seasonal color, I planted crocuses, daffodils, blue salvias, pale yellow *Coreopsis* 'Moonbeam' and the black-eyed Susan *Rudbeckia* 'Goldsturm'. Several plants provide horticultural drama. In spring, bold color comes from the yellow or red bracts of *Euphorbia myrsinites*, *E. wulfenii*, and *E. griffithii* 'Fireglow'. In summer, crambe (*Crambe cordifolia*) sends up 6-ft. tall flowering stems that look like giant baby's-breath.

The bank has been largely a success, with a few educational mistakes. The miscanthus, which are huge grasses, shed water like a thatched roof, so nothing grows at their feet. Unfortunately, like all upright grasses, miscanthus are least attractive around

their feet, and to make matters even worse, mine are planted at eye level. I need to plant many more midsize grasses—perhaps varieties of fountain grass, except *Pennisetum setaceum* 'Rubrum', which is not hardy here. Nonetheless, 'Rubrum' is worth growing as an annual just to watch the children playing with the pink tassels.

Some parts of the bank are so dry nothing has grown there. My only success was accidental—a clump of

A wisteria-covered trellis and a board fence shelter a private patio in a corner of the backyard. The huge leaves of gunnera rise above a formal pool where a fountain yields the sound of splashing water. (Photo taken at D.)

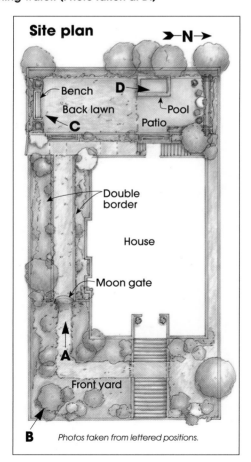

Site plan

N

Bench

Back lawn

D

Pool

C

Patio

Double border

House

Moon gate

A

Front yard

B

Photos taken from lettered positions.

Carex buchananii. It has brown-bronze leaves, and when it died it still looked the same as it did when alive.

The grasses are at their best in the fall, thrashing around like an angry sea in the whirling wind. They add an exuberance and drama no other plants can match. But grooming is a problem. Always they push a somewhat tidy man to the limit. When is a grass drying picturesquely and when is it untended debris? The leaves pull loose and start flying around in February's winds. Then I usually decide enough is enough and cut the grasses to within a few inches of the ground. I always find the spring bulbs interplanted nearby are already 6-in. tall.

How the design matured

In early spring last year, I thought the garden was perfect. Two weeks later, with the plants in full leaf, I thought it was a disaster. Some of the shrubs had grown too large; some plants had disappeared or declined; and some plants no longer pleased me. It was time to renovate the perennial beds. Four years is a long time for intensely planted beds. The soil needs amending. Plants get crowded and weary and need to be dug up, divided and replanted. I'm looking forward to the renovation. The main bed by the lawn will be first, and every year I will do another.

The pond never did turn into a sandbox. It has been a wading pool during warm weather and a source of fascination for all children. We have to be constantly vigilant, of course, to make sure no one falls in, but it's worth the effort. The neighborhood raccoons demolished any fish or plants we put into the pool, though, so we quickly gave up on them.

The garden gets a lot of use. I've taught children to respect the plants, and the plants have been very forgiving about tossed balls. The wisteria has finally bloomed. One unexpected reward happened at my daughter's pre-school when the teacher brought in a bouquet. All the children cried out "flowers." All except my daughter, that is, who said, "Daffodils, tulips, irises, pansies and roses." □

Douglas Bayley is a landscape designer in Seattle, Washington.

Illustration: Rosalind Loeb Wanke

An Illusion of Age

Unrestrained plantings and weathered masonry bring a timeworn feel to a formal city garden

A quiet garden in a noisy city setting. The rubble-filled basement of a demolished house was paved over and walled in to create a private garden next to the author's house. Photo taken at **A** on Site Plan, p. 92.

By Gary Ross

My new garden has the overgrown look of an old garden. Its plants grow naturally, spilling over the edges of their borders. The result is a slightly unkempt and ageless-looking landscape (see top photo on p. 91) that suits the architecture of my venerable brick house.

The street facade of the 87-year-old Georgian revival house is symmetrical, with windows equally spaced on either side of a centered front door. But the back of the house is completely different—a collection of variously sized room additions and asymmetrically placed windows. The gardens, like the house, are a collection of rooms, both formal and informal in design.

My neighborhood, an inner-city area of Columbus, has houses situated close together with small front and

All photos: George C. Anderson

back yards; there was only 3 ft. between my house and neighboring houses. At the time, neither the size of my yard nor the desire to garden was a consideration—I bought the house because it was big and the location was convenient. As a sculptor who makes life-size and larger figures, I needed a lot of work space. The house had three-and-a-half stories plus a basement, and it was close to the university where I teach art.

When I did get around to working in the yard, I found it neglected and surprisingly overgrown for its size. Before I could conceive of a garden, I had to remove truckloads of mulberry trees, wild grapevines, trumpet vines and other undesirable plants.

The front-yard garden

My street was once lined with mature Dutch elm trees, but blight wiped them out, leaving an empty slate of a front yard. I decided to keep it simple, furnishing it with neatly growing and formally trimmed plants to echo the architecture of the house.

First, I laid a 7-ft.-wide, straight brick walk in the middle of the front yard, from the street to the front door. I lined the walk with hostas *(H. undulata)*, and planted clipped yew hedges *(Taxus × media* 'Hicksii') at the base of the white-columned porch (see Site Plan on p. 92), finishing the front yard with a few well-placed trees. A little-leaf linden *(Tilia cordata)* visually balances a tree in my neighbor's front yard, and one flowering dogwood tree *(Cornus florida)* on each side of the brick walk marks the point where it meets the street.

The garden grows

My garden began to expand nine years ago when I tore down an unsound house to the west of my property. When the house went, so did the plants that grew around it, but I salvaged building materials to use in a new garden. When the demolition was over, I had bricks and stones, and an empty lot that was separated into three sections, each with varying degrees of garden promise.

I envisioned an expanded front yard and three garden rooms, each

▲ **A young garden with a venerable look:** The author gave his property a patina of age by allowing its plants to grow with untrimmed abandon. Photo taken at **B.**

◄ **Warming up early spring.** Pink-flowered Japanese Higan cherry trees add warmth and color to the green hosta-lined pool and grassy court beyond. Photo taken at **C.**

with a distinct look and palette of plants. The front yard of the former house still had grass, so, to make it part of my own front yard, I simply replaced the front walk with sod.

The former basement, which covered an area parallel to and almost as long as my house, was filled in with "clean fill." I thought, mistakenly, that clean fill would be topsoil in which I could garden. It turned out that clean fill is mostly chunks of cement, blacktop and gravel with very little soil.

At the back of the lot, the demolition crew had churned up the soil with the machines they used to tear down the house. With the topsoil stripped away, orange Ohio clay was all that was left there. After sizing up the situation, I faced the challenge of creating new gardens.

The walled garden

I solved the problem of the rubble-filled basement by paving it and surrounding it with walls to create a formal walled garden. Adding 10 ft. to the foundation on the west side of the former house made it the same length as my house. I built a 6-ft.-tall brick wall on the foundation, and a 6-ft.-tall curved brick wall across the front of the lot, connecting the side wall to my house.

To blend the wall into my expanded front yard, I lined the front of the wall with hydrangeas (*H. arborescens* 'Grandiflora') and more hostas. To balance the trees in the front yard, I planted a purple-leaf weeping beech tree (*Fagus sylvatica* 'Purpurea Pendula') in the new front yard (see Site Plan, above).

The planting area within the walled garden is small, but by planting compact and upright plants, I created a garden rich in variety. I began by training plants to cover the walls with flowers and foliage to extend their height for privacy. A weeping Japanese Higan cherry (*Prunus subhirtella*) fills each of the four corners of the walled garden with pale pink flowers in spring and cascading foliage in summer and fall.

To hide the inside front of the wall, I planted American arborvitaes (*Thuja occidentalis*) and more yews in the two corners fac-

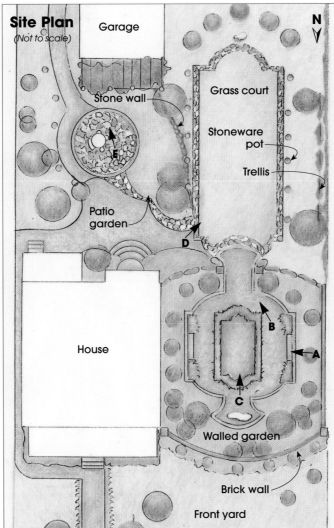

Site Plan
(Not to scale)
Garage
Stone wall
Grass court
Stoneware pot
Trellis
Patio garden
House
E
D
B
A
C
Walled garden
Brick wall
Front yard
N

A grassy patch opens up a small garden.
The lawn is brightened by borders of brick and stone, and stoneware planters made by the author. Photo taken at **D.**

ing the street and along the wall. A grapevine (*Vitis labrusca* 'Concord'), silver-lace vines (*Polygonum aubertii*) and wisterias (*W. floribunda*) drape the front wall and part of the side wall with fragrant flowers in spring, and foliage through summer and fall. Two hornbeams (*Carpinus betulus* 'Fastigiata') and boxwoods (*Buxus sempervirens*) hide my basement windows (see photo on p. 90). Three columnar English oaks (*Quercus robur* 'Fastigiata') on the west wall screen my neighbor's house.

I separated the walled garden, which occupies the space formerly covered by the neighboring house, from its former back yard with a row of arborvitaes. The evergreens form a curve that repeats the shape of the front wall. A central walk leads from the former back yard into the walled garden between two posts that I built from salvaged limestone blocks. I topped the stone pillars with clematis (*C. × jackmanii*) and with satyrs, those mythical creatures of revelry, which I sculpted. I planted clematis at the base of the pillars so that it would wrap the satyrs in flowery garlands. I put two more of these sculptures on corner posts of the brick wall, where their mischievous smiles can be glimpsed from the front yard.

The walled garden is laid out around a central walk, or axis, echoing the formal layout of my front yard. When entering the garden between the two stone posts, a hosta-bordered reflecting pool planted with 'White Sultan' water lilies lies straight ahead (see bottom photo on p. 91). The pool is shaped like the curved, Palladian windows in the front and back of my house, and its 3-ft. depth keeps goldfish from freezing in winter. I bordered the pool with a walk made of crushed brick to introduce the color of the house and wall into the garden. The graceful, curving foliage of grasslike liriope (*L. spicata*) borders the walks. The space between the walk and the walls is filled with flowering perennials, including hostas, English ivy, periwinkle, sweet woodruff and pachysandra.

As accents, I placed wooden benches and impatiens-filled ceramic planters, which I made, on each side of the pool (see photo on p. 90). The focal point of the walled garden is a life-size, bronze seated male figure that I sculpted and centered between the pool and the the curved wall.

The grass court

After I finished the walled garden, I created a grassy court from what had been the back yard next door (see photo on p.92). At the rear of the court I displayed a standing female figure on a limestone and cement pedestal. A row of upright white pines (*Pinus strobus* 'Pyramidalis') behind the sculpture screen utility poles and wires.

Along the west side of the court I set up a row of five arched wrought-iron trellises, each 6 ft. wide and 8 ft. tall. They support bittersweet, rose and clematis vines. Behind the trellises, I planted a screen of pussy willows (*Salix caprea*), dawn redwoods (*Metasequoia glyptostroboides*) and redbuds (*Cercis canadensis*).

An old garage gets a new face. Shiny, mirrored "windows" and a pillared arbor with cascading wisteria add pizzazz to the author's old garage and the new patio garden beside it. Photo taken at **E**.

The paved garden

The back yard was the last garden I built. This garden is slightly higher than the adjoining grassy court, so I put a stone retaining wall between them. The back of my house has room additions and a porch, and there is an old, freestanding garage at the back of the yard. I decided to make the space between these random structures into an informal garden.

Paving unites the various parts of this garden. I dubbed the patchwork patterns and irregular surfaces of my paving efforts my "landwrap" method of paving. First, I built a semicircular landing and steps of salvaged brick leading from my dining-room door into the new garden. Then, from the base of the steps, I paved much of the area with bricks in a running pat-

tern, allowing them to follow the changing contour of the ground (see photo, above). For interest, I used Pennsylvania flagstone to pave a round pattern in the center of the area, and bordered it with bricks.

Then came the finishing touch. I decided to dress up the old garage by putting white columns on the front of it to match those on the front porch of the house. These garage columns support a wisteria-covered arbor, which provides a fragrant backdrop for the sitting area. I attached 7-ft.-tall mirrors to the garage wall between each column—these make-believe Palladian windows reflect the garden, making it look larger.

For privacy, I added a border between the patio and a neighbor's fence. Maple trees and honeysuckle

bushes were already growing there— I just filled in around them with English ivy, tulips, periwinkle and hostas. Then I planted a purple-leaf plum tree (*Prunus cerasifera* 'Atropurpurea') to add a spot of color to the otherwise green background. Six of my stoneware planters accent the edge of the paved area.

Now that my gardens are finished, I retreat to them to relax when I'm not teaching or working on sculptures. Each day I notice that some plants are getting ready to bloom, some are blooming already, and some have flowers that are fading. I look forward to watching my gardens change. ∎

Gary Ross is a sculptor and professor of fine arts at Capital University in Columbus, Ohio.

Index

O

Overy, Angela, on walled garden in Colorado, 39-43

P

Paths. *See* Walkways.
Patios:
  brick, 12, 60-61, 62
  covered, 48, 52
  as garden rooms, 79
  multilevel, 14-17
  for small city backyard, 37, 38
  walled, front-yard, 24-27
  in walled garden, 39-40, 41
  See also Courtyards.
Paving:
  materials for, 20
  for patio garden, 93
Perennials, for alpine landscape, 84-85
Pergolas:
  as ceilings for garden rooms, 10
  for Southwest garden, 52
  wisteria-covered, 64, 65
  See also Trellises.
Petunias, for courtyard garden, 71
Planters:
  brick, 60-61
  ceramic, as garden accents, 93
  landscape-tie, as room dividers, 15, 16
Plants:
  for containers, 71-73
  as garden walls, 9
  for small city garden, 88-89
  for small tropical garden, 74-79
Pollarding, as pruning technique, 47
Ponds:
  in enclosed front yard, 62
  for small backyard, 13
  in Southwest garden, 51, 52
  waterfall, in small tropical garden, 77
Pools, reflecting:
  for formal walled garden, 92-93
  narrow, for walled front yard, 25, 26-27
  in small city garden, 87-88
Pots. *See* Containers.
Proctor, Rob, on communal courtyard garden, 68-73
Purple smoke tree *(Cotinus coggyrgia* 'Purpureus'), pruning, 47

R

Raised beds:
  for Southwest garden, 50, 51
  stone, 80, 81-82
  for townhouse garden, 34
  See also Planters.
Ross, Gary, on timeworn city garden, 90-93

S

Sheldon, Elisabeth, on bold-colored flowers, 18-23
Shrubs, for garden screening, 44-47
Stairs, in multilevel garden, 17
Stone:
  for garden floors, 10
  for garden walls, 24-27

T

Trees, for garden screening, 44-47
Trellises:
  over pond, 60, 62
  wisteria-covered, 81, 82, 87, 88, 89
  wrought-iron, as vine support, 93
  See also Pergolas.

V

Vines, for garden enclosure, 54-57

W

Walkways:
  brick, 58, 62, 91, 92-93
    plants for, 52
  entry, brick and concrete, 24, 26
  in formal/informal garden, 64-67
  timber-step, 74, 76, 78
Walls:
  brick, for enclosed city garden, 92
  for entry gardens, 9-10
  stone,
    for front-yard retreat, 25, 26
    for raised beds, 81-82
  stucco, for enclosed garden, 39, 40, 41, 43
Waterfalls, in small tropical garden, 75, 77
Waterways:
  in alpine landscape, 85
  in formal/informal garden, 66-67
Wildlife, in Southwest garden, 51

The 19 articles in this book originally appeared in *Fine Gardening* magazine.
The date of first publication, issue number and page numbers for each article are given below.